W9-BYD-743

People in the NEWS

Mark
Zuckerberg

Mark
Zuckerberg

By: Mary E. Williams

LUCENT BOOKS
A part of Gale, Cengage Learning

GALE
CENGAGE Learning·

Detroit • New York • San Francisco • New Haven, Conn • Waterville, Maine • London

Library of Congress Cataloging-in-Publication Data

Williams, Mary E., 1960-
  Mark Zuckerberg / by Mary E. Williams.
    p. cm. -- (People in the news)
  Includes bibliographical references and index.
  ISBN 978-1-4205-0758-4 (hardcover)
 1. Zuckerberg, Mark, 1984- 2. Facebook (Firm) 3. Facebook (Electronic resource)
 4. Businesspeople--United States--Biography. 5. Online social networks.
 6. Webmasters--United States--Biography. I. Title.
  HM743.F33W55 2013
  302.30285092--dc23
  [B]

2012024872

Lucent Books
27500 Drake Rd
Farmington Hills MI 48331

ISBN-13: 978-1-4205-0758-4
ISBN-10: 1-4205-0758-3

Printed in the United States of America
1 2 3 4 5 6 7 16 15 14 13 12

Contents

Fame and celebrity are alluring. People are drawn to those who walk in fame's spotlight, whether they are known for great accomplishments or for notorious deeds. The lives of the famous pique public interest and attract attention, perhaps because their experiences seem in some ways so different from, yet in other ways so similar to, our own.

Newspapers, magazines, and television regularly capitalize on this fascination with celebrity by running profiles of famous people. For example, television programs such as *Entertainment Tonight* devote all their programming to stories about entertainment and entertainers. Magazines such as *People* fill their pages with stories of the private lives of famous people. Even newspapers, newsmagazines, and television news frequently delve into the lives of well-known personalities. Despite the number of articles and programs, few provide more than a superficial glimpse at their subjects.

Lucent's People in the News series offers young readers a deeper look into the lives of today's newsmakers, the influences that have shaped them, and the impact they have had in their fields of endeavor and on other people's lives. The subjects of the series hail from many disciplines and walks of life. They include authors, musicians, athletes, political leaders, entertainers, entrepreneurs, and others who have made a mark on modern life and who, in many cases, will continue to do so for years to come.

These biographies are more than factual chronicles. Each book emphasizes the contributions, accomplishments, or deeds that have brought fame or notoriety to the individual and shows how that person has influenced modern life. Authors portray their subjects in a realistic, unsentimental light. For example, Bill Gates—cofounder of the software giant Microsoft—has been instrumental in making personal computers the most vital tool of the modern age. Few dispute his business savvy, his perseverance, or his technical expertise, yet critics say he is ruthless in his dealings with competitors and driven more by his desire to maintain Microsoft's dominance in the computer industry than by an interest in furthering technology.

In these books, young readers will encounter inspiring stories about real people who achieved success despite enormous obstacles. Oprah Winfrey—one of the most powerful, most watched, and wealthiest women in television history—spent the first six years of her life in the care of her grandparents while her unwed mother sought work and a better life elsewhere. Her adolescence was colored by pregnancy at age fourteen, rape, and sexual abuse.

Each author documents and supports his or her work with an array of primary and secondary source quotations taken from diaries, letters, speeches, and interviews. All quotes are footnoted to show readers exactly how and where biographers derive their information and provide guidance for further research. The quotations enliven the text by giving readers eyewitness views of the life and accomplishments of each person covered in the People in the News series.

In addition, each book in the series includes photographs, annotated bibliographies, timelines, and comprehensive indexes. For both the casual reader and the student researcher, the People in the News series offers insight into the lives of today's newsmakers—people who shape the way we live, work, and play in the modern age.

A Rogue Who Builds Bridges

On June 9, 2011, twenty-seven-year-old Mark Zuckerberg gave a brief speech to the graduating class at Belle Haven Community School in Menlo Park, California. Although he could not recall very much about his own middle school graduation, he said there was one person who stood out in his memory. His favorite teacher, Mr. Walsh, was missing one eye and always wore an eye patch. Zuckerberg recounted that the pre-elementary students would point at the teacher and say, "Hey, look—a pirate!" The teacher would look back at them and say, "Yes, pirate—argh!"[1]

At age nineteen, when Zuckerberg was a sophomore at Harvard University, he became a pirate of sorts himself. Somewhat intoxicated and upset after an argument with a young woman, he spent a night hacking into the university's computer network to retrieve the ID pictures of students living on campus. He used them to create a website called Facemash, which allowed viewers to compare the head shots of two students and vote on which one was more attractive. Facemash spread around campus so quickly that it caught the attention of Harvard's computer services department, which shut off Zuckerberg's web access a few hours after the site's launch. Zuckerberg was charged with breach of security, copyright infringement, and violation of privacy. Harvard's disciplinary board placed him on probation.

Little did anyone know that this sophomoric prank would lay the groundwork for a revolution in social media. The Facemash fiasco contained the seed of an idea that catapulted Zuckerberg into another project: creating an online and interactive version of the house photo directories, or facebooks, that on-campus students received at the beginning of the school year. After reading the criticisms of Facemash that appeared in campus newspaper editorials and wanting to apologize for any offense his actions caused, Zuckerberg constructed a social network for the university community. He launched this network, then known as TheFacebook, from his dorm room on February 4, 2004.

A Meteoric Rise

In just eight years Facebook transformed from a bare-bones website used by a few Ivy League students to a sophisticated public networking platform with more than 800 million global members—one out of every nine people on the planet. It is the most visited social network in the world, and it has made

Zuckerberg poses at the Facebook offices in 2007. In its first eight years, Facebook grew to include 800 million members worldwide and earned Zuckerberg a personal fortune of $17.5 billion.

Zuckerberg, with an estimated $17.5 billion in personal wealth, one of the youngest multibillionaires in the world.

Yet Zuckerberg never set out to run a company and become immensely wealthy. He maintains that he simply loves writing computer code and making technological tools that help people learn, share, and connect more with each other. As such, he sees himself—and Facebook—as expressing the spirit of his generation, which was shaped by the information revolution of the late twentieth century. Zuckerberg explains in an interview:

> I'm in the first generation of people who really grew up with the Internet. Google came out when I was in middle school. Then there was Amazon and Wikipedia and iTunes and Napster. Each year, there were new ways to access information. Now you can look up anything you want. Now you can get cool reference material. Now you can download any song you want. Now you can get directions to anything. The world kept on getting better and better.[2]

Zuckerberg is a shining example of an optimist. He says Facebook's mission is "to make the world more open and connected" and believes that values such as empathy, accountability, and integrity emerge naturally when people are given more ways to share and relate to each other. The past, in contrast, offered fewer opportunities for these values to find expression. "If you go back, most people in the world had no voice, or they had no podium where they could share things. But now everyone does,"[3] says Zuckerberg.

Not everyone agrees that Zuckerberg simply wants to build bridges between people. Former colleagues accused him of stealing the idea for Facebook from their social network. Privacy advocates questioned Zuckerberg's motives when Facebook began tracking users' web-surfing habits, sharing that information with advertisers, and even, for a brief time, broadcasting members' purchases to their network of friends. Moreover, a popular 2010 movie depicting the founding of Facebook painted Zuckerberg as an envious nerd driven by the need to prove himself to the cool crowd. Zuckerberg resented this portrayal. "It's interesting—the stuff they focused on getting right," he commented. "Every single shirt or fleece in the movie is actually a shirt or fleece that I own … [but] they just can't wrap their head around the idea that someone might build something because they like building things."[4]

Changing the Way the World Communicates

Zuckerberg's delight in building tools has undoubtedly transformed how people communicate with each other. Today many prefer Facebook to e-mail as a way to contact friends and family online. Others use it to share photos, videos, music, and links to news stories, editorials, blogs, or other sites. Most users log in at least once a day to write a pithy update, see what their friends are up to, converse with members of a group, play games, or send gifts. Just a decade ago, there were no social networks that offered such a variety of easily accessible ways to connect and communicate with others.

In pondering how far he and his company cofounders have come, Zuckerberg seems grateful, and even slightly bemused, about Facebook's role in the world:

> I remember hanging out with my friends [at] the local pizza place, talking about [how] in the future, you're going to be able to share all the stuff that you want and you're going to … have access to all of these different experiences. But we just figured that someone else was going to do it. I mean, who were *we* to go build this? …We were nineteen years old, we were in college, we knew *nothing* about companies. … Who'd have thought it, right?[5]

Chapter 1

Boy Wonder

Mark Elliot Zuckerberg was born on May 14, 1984, at a hospital in White Plains, New York, to Edward (Ed) and Karen Zuckerberg, a Jewish couple. They lived in Dobbs Ferry, New York, a village just north of New York City, in the affluent suburban county of Westchester. At the time of Mark's birth, he had one older sister, Randi, but more Zuckerberg children were on the way. Mark, the sole boy among four siblings, also has two younger sisters: Donna and Arielle. Because he was the only son, Mark was nicknamed "the Prince."

A Supportive Family

Ed ran a dental practice in the basement of the family's large house. Also known as "painless Dr. Z," Ed liked using funny mottoes to attract patients, such as "we cater to cowards" and "be true to your teeth or they will be false to you."[6] Karen left her job as a psychiatrist after the birth of the couple's first child and became a stay-at-home mom and an office manager for her husband's practice.

Ed had grown up as the son of a Brooklyn, New York, mail carrier whose "method of fixing a TV that went out of whack was to take a fist and pop it,"[7] according to Mark. Ed took an entirely different approach to modern equipment as a teen: He enjoyed taking stereos apart just to see how they worked.

Mark also had the same inquisitive, analytical nature that his father had displayed in his own youth. Ed describes Mark as "strong-willed and relentless" as a young boy. While many young children are satisfied with yes or no answers to their questions, "If [Mark] asked for something, *yes* by itself would work, but *no* required much more," Ed remembers. "If you were going to say no to him, you had better be prepared with a strong argument backed by facts, experiences, logic, reasons. We envisioned him becoming a lawyer one day, with a near 100% success rate of convincing juries."[8]

The Zuckerbergs were strongly committed to encouraging their children to develop their particular talents and to follow their dreams. "Rather than impose upon your kids or try and steer their lives in a certain direction, [it is important] to … support the development of the things they're passionate about,"[9] says Ed. Mark's talent for out-of-the-box thinking emerged early in a supportive household that valued education, skill, and creativity.

Surrounded by Computers

Mark's analytical skills eventually became focused on computers and technology. The first Macintosh Apple computer was launched in 1984, the year Mark was born. That same year, his father purchased his first office computer, a huge IBM XT. Although it did little more than print out invoices, Ed relished it: "It wasn't about the math; it was about the vision."[10]

By 1985 the entire Zuckerberg home and office were computerized. Ed himself had a limited background in computer science, but he enjoyed acquiring the latest technological gadgets for his practice as well as for recreation. All four of the Zuckerberg children were given their own computers. This proved to be a boon for Mark, who had become bored with his schoolwork. "There are advantages to being exposed to computers early on," notes Ed. "That certainly enriched Mark's interest in technology."[11]

Among the high-tech devices that Ed bought was an early Atari 800, one of the first home computers. Resembling a large electric typewriter, the machine came with a disk that enabled Mark to learn a version of BASIC (beginner's all-purpose

The IBM XT was a type of personal computer used in the early 1980s. It was the first computer that Zuckerberg's father purchased to use in his dental office in 1984.

symbolic instruction code), a computer programming language. The Zuckerbergs also gave Mark the book *C++ for Dummies*, an introduction to programming. When he was nearly eleven years old, Mark's parents hired David Newman, a software developer, to tutor Mark at home once a week. "He was a prodigy," Newman claims. "Sometimes it was tough to stay ahead of him."[12]

In addition to Newman's tutoring, Mark began attending graduate computer courses at nearby Mercy College once a week. Mark's young age was a surprise to his classmates and his teachers there. When Ed dropped him off for his first class, the instructor looked at Ed and said, motioning to Mark, "You can't bring him to the classroom with you."[13] Ed had to explain that it was the boy who was taking the class.

What Is C++?

Mark Zuckerberg received a copy of the book *C++ for Dummies* from his parents when he was ten years old. The text gives the following definition of C++, a general-purpose computer programming language:

> A computer is an amazingly fast but incredibly stupid machine. A computer can do anything you tell it (within reason), but it does *exactly* what it's told—nothing more and nothing less. ...
>
> Computers understand a language variously known as *computer language* or *machine language*. It's possible but extremely difficult for humans to speak machine language. Therefore, computers and humans have agreed to sort of meet in the middle, using intermediate languages such as C++. Humans can speak C++ (sort of), and C++ can be converted into machine language for the computer to understand.

Stephen R. Davis. *C++ for Dummies.* 6th ed. Hoboken, NJ: Wiley, 2009, p. 9.

Early on, Mark had inventive skills and a penchant for creating tools to get things done faster. One day in 1996, when Mark was almost twelve, he heard his father say that he wished there were a better way of announcing a patient's arrival than having the receptionist yell down from upstairs. Using the Atari BASIC computer language, Mark created a messaging software program that enabled all the Zuckerberg home and office computers to communicate with each other. The family named it "Zucknet." Professionals were brought in to do the wiring of Zucknet, as home computer networks were basically unheard of at that time. Zucknet was, in essence, a primitive version of America Online's (AOL's) Instant Messenger, which did not come out until the following year.

Imaginative Play

Mark's taste for computers and other new gadgets also had a dreamy, playful side. His favorite movies were the first three installments (episodes 4–6) of the *Star Wars* film series. This science-fiction and fantasy series is full of special effects and visionary technologies. One year, during a wintertime school break, Mark and his sisters decided to film a complete parody of *Star Wars*. They named it *The Star Wars Sill-ogy*. "We took our job very seriously," his sister Randi says. "Every morning we'd wake up and have production meetings. Mark's voice hadn't changed yet, so he played [the protagonist] Luke Skywalker with a really high, squeaky voice, and then my little sister, who I think was 2, we stuck her in a garbage can as [robot] R2-D2 and had her walk around."[14] When he turned thirteen, Mark's bar mitzvah ceremony (a coming of age ceremony for Jewish boys) had a *Star Wars* theme.

Pranks and practical jokes were a part of life in the Zuckerberg home. One night Mark's sister Donna was working on her computer in her room downstairs. Mark turned to Randi and said, "I bet I can make Donna come upstairs in five seconds."[15] He rigged things so that a screen popped up on Donna's computer, warning her that she had downloaded a deadly virus that would cause the computer to self-destruct in thirty seconds. The machine began counting down, and up the stairs Donna ran, yelling, "Mark!"[16] Later, in 1999, the Zuckerberg parents were, like much of the computer-using world at the time, worried about the Y2K (Year 2000) bug, a potential massive failure among computers that many feared would occur when the year rolled over from 1999 to 2000. One main concern was that there might be widespread blackouts. On New Year's Eve 1999, Mark and Randi waited until the stroke of midnight, then secretly shut off the electrical power to the house. Despite this prank, the widespread havoc from Y2K that many people around the world were anticipating never materialized.

Twenty-first century technologies held great appeal for Mark's circle of friends. Many of them loved to play computer games. Mark went further: He loved to write programming code for computer games. He created a version of the board game Monopoly—with

The Star Wars films were a favorite of Zuckerberg when he was a child. He played Luke Skywalker in a parody of the movie he once made with his sisters.

his middle school as the setting—as well as a variation on the board game Risk. "It was centered around the ancient Roman Empire," Mark explains. "You played against Julius Caesar. He was good, and I was never able to win."[17] Mark also gained inspiration for coding from friends of his who were artists: "They'd come over, draw stuff, and I'd build a game out of it."[18]

Transferring to a Prep School

For much of his childhood, Mark attended local public schools. He enrolled at Ardsley High School, a place not far from his home, where he excelled in classics: the languages, history, and culture of ancient Greece and ancient Rome. As well as he did at Ardsley, however, Mark transferred to Phillips Exeter Academy, an elite private school, after his sophomore year. Ardsley did not offer many computer or higher math courses, and Mark's parents wanted to boost his chances of being admitted to an Ivy League college.

The Phillips Exeter Academy is an elite prep school in New Hampshire that Zuckerberg attended for his last two years of high school.

Phillips Exeter Academy

Established in 1781, Phillips Exeter Academy is a coed boarding school located in rural New Hampshire. Exeter is noted for using the Harkness Method, a seminar style of learning in which eight to twelve students sit around a large, oval table with a teacher who instructs them through conferences and tutorials, encouraging each person to actively participate. There are no lectures, no traditional textbooks, and no classrooms containing rows of desks. Approaches to teaching different subjects vary, but the main goal is to have students come up with ideas of their own and to practice good critical-thinking and discussion skills. In some cases teachers speak hardly at all, interjecting only to guide the class discussion.

Famous Exeter alumni include U.S. president Franklin Pierce, U.S. senator Jay Rockefeller, businessperson Joseph Coors, and the authors Gore Vidal, John Irving, and Dan Brown.

Exeter provided a more challenging environment for an eager and inventive mind like Mark's. His required coursework included art, classical and modern languages, computer science, math, health and human development, history, religion, and science. Mark won prizes in math, astronomy, and physics; he also excelled in literature, classics, and Latin. Although he jokingly claimed that he only preferred Latin and other ancient languages because he spoke modern foreign languages with a poor accent, Mark had tentative plans to study classics at Harvard after finishing high school. Exeter's highly regarded Latin program would provide a strong foundation for college-level classics.

A Well-Rounded Education

Mark's achievements and experiences during his time at Exeter extended beyond the academic, however. As one interviewer quips, "Mark was not a stereotypical geek-klutz."[19] He played in

Students work at the library at the Phillips Exeter Academy. In addition to the school's academic rigors, Zuckerberg also experienced its emphasis on strong social ties.

the school band. In addition, after being voted the year 2000's most valuable player at the New York regional competition of the U.S. Fencing Association (USFA), Mark became captain of the Exeter fencing team. He saw fencing as "the perfect medium" because "whether I am competing against a rival in a USFA tournament or just clashing foils [fencing swords], or sometimes sabers, with a friend, I rarely find myself doing anything more enjoyable than fencing a good bout."[20] Still, Mark continued toying with inventive projects, creating new conveniences for the people around him. With his classmate Kristopher Tillery, for example, he set up a website that allowed Exeter students to order snacks online.

Mark's time at prep school also exposed him to a lifestyle that emphasized strong social ties. As writer Steffan Antonas notes, "Exeter's tight-knit boarding community lives on campus full-time. Students think of themselves as 'Exonians' and have a strong group identity rooted in a rich culture of customs and tradition."[21] For many years part of this tradition included receiving an annual edition of the school's student directory. When Mark enrolled at Exeter at the beginning of his junior year, he and all the other students were given a copy of this directory. Its cover title was *The Photo Address Book*, but students referred to it as "the Facebook" because that was less of a mouthful.

As the name suggests, Exeter's Facebook contained the names, photos, campus house addresses, and contact information of each student. Such photo directories were (and still are) a significant part of social life at many prep schools. With cell phones banned on campus and students' living accommodations changing from year to year, the school's Facebook was a well-appreciated resource. As Antonas points out: "Not only do students need the directory to find and contact their peers, but the books become part of the culture of bonding between classmates and friends, as students use it to see where their peers live, who's hot and who's not, who lives with who, and who the new kids are."[22]

In 2002, when Mark was a senior, the student council successfully lobbied the school administration to launch an online version of the Exeter Facebook. Mark was not involved with this development, however. His attention was increasingly drawn to innovative computer programming experiments. Exeter's Computer Science Division invited students "to reexamine their views on technology's place in the modern world, reevaluate the limitations of computers, and reorganize their own thinking to best combine the creativity of humans with the efficiency and precision of computers."[23] Accordingly, Mark embarked on an ambitious senior project with his classmate and friend Adam D'Angelo.

A Huge Offer

For their project, Mark and Adam formed a real company named Intelligent Media Group and created Synapse Media Player, a software program that was able to build a digital library based on a user's musical tastes. As Mark explains, "It learned your listening

Before he became a technology executive, Adam D'Angelo was Zuckerberg's classmate at Exeter. The two started their first company together while still in high school.

patterns by figuring out how much you like each song at a given point of time, and which songs you tend to listen to around each other."[24] He and Adam posted about Synapse on Slashdot, a technology-related website, and offered it as a free download. News about the groundbreaking software spread quickly among technology bloggers, and *PC Magazine* gave it a rating of 3 out of 5.

Soon several large companies, including Microsoft and AOL, expressed an interest in recruiting the two youths and in purchasing Synapse. "Some companies offered us right off the bat up to one million, and then we got another offer that was like two million,"[25] Mark recounts. However, Mark and Adam turned the offers down, opting to attend college instead. Months later, when they were both college students, Mark and Adam changed their mind and decided to take the $2 million offer on Synapse, but by then the offer had expired. "We were pretty naïve about it,"[26] Mark says.

Mark graduated from Exeter with a classics diploma in the spring of 2002. In his college application, he listed that he could read and write French, Hebrew, Latin, and ancient Greek. He was a fencing champion, a math whiz, and had already acquired, by the young age of eighteen, a reputation as a skilled computer programmer and technological trendsetter. Mark was accepted by Harvard University and moved to the prestigious Cambridge, Massachusetts, campus in the autumn of 2002.

Chapter 2

Hacking and High Jinks at Harvard

Mark Zuckerberg arrived at Harvard in September 2002 with a reputation as a programming prodigy. He decided to major in both computer science and psychology—the latter reflecting an interest in his mother's field of expertise. He joined Alpha Epsilon Pi, a Jewish fraternity.

Initially, Zuckerberg did not really stand out in a crowd of his peers. At one of the country's most elite universities, he was surrounded by hundreds of other bright freshmen who were also talented and ambitious. At 5 feet 8 inches, with a slender build, freckled face, and curly brown hair, he appeared a little younger than his eighteen years. He tended to wear baggy jeans, rubber flip-flops—even in winter—and T-shirts with witty phrases or images. One of his favorite T-shirts at this time had a drawing of a small ape with the words "Code Monkey."

The Irreverent Geek

As an introvert and a deliberate thinker, Zuckerberg tended to be quiet around strangers. According to author David Kirkpatrick, however, this quietness was deceiving:

> When he did speak, he was wry. His tendency was to say nothing until others fully had their say. He stared. He would stare at you while you were talking, and stay absolutely silent. If you said something stimulating, he'd finally fire up his own

ideas and the words would come cascading out. But if you went on too long or said something obvious, he would start looking through you. When you finished, he'd quietly mutter "yeah," then change the subject or turn away.[27]

Zuckerberg seemed to embrace a standoffish, geeky personality, but he also enjoyed parties. At one of the Friday night parties at his fraternity, he met the woman who would later become his long-term girlfriend, Priscilla Chan. As they stood in a line outside of the restroom, the two chatted. "He was this nerdy guy

Harvard University

Established in 1636, Harvard University is the oldest institution of higher education in the United States. Harvard College, its undergraduate school, has an average of sixty-four hundred students each year. Freshmen live in one of the Harvard Yard dormitories; after completing their first year, students reside in one of the twelve houses on campus, guided by a

The campus of historic Harvard University is in Cambridge, Massachusetts.

resident master and staff of tutors. Ninety-seven percent of undergrads live on campus, creating a strong sense of campus community. The college boasts numerous famous graduates, such as U.S. president John F. Kennedy, composer Yo-Yo Ma, and actress Natalie Portman. It also has some well-known dropouts, including actor Matt Damon, Microsoft founder Bill Gates, and Facebook creator Mark Zuckerberg.

who was just a little bit out there," Chan recalls. "I remember he had these beer glasses that said 'pound include beer dot H.' It's a tag for C++. It's like college humor but with a nerdy, computer-science appeal."[28]

Underneath an aloof exterior, Zuckerberg was full of ideas, self-confidence, and mischief. During his stint at Harvard, his brilliance and persistence would bring him recognition even as his occasional misbehavior got him into trouble.

A Sloppy Suite

At the beginning of his sophomore year, Zuckerberg was living in one of the smallest four-person suites in Kirkland House, a Harvard dorm. Each suite contained two bedrooms joined by a common room, where all four suitemates had their own work desk. Zuckerberg was rooming with Chris Hughes, a history and

Kirkland House is the dorm on the Harvard University campus where Zuckerberg lived when he began programming the website that became Facebook.

literature major interested in public policy. Dustin Moskovitz, an economics major, and Billy Olson, a theater enthusiast, lived in the other half of the suite.

The bedrooms were designed to fit bunk beds and one small desk. Zuckerberg and Hughes, deciding that neither of them wanted to sleep on the top bunk, dismantled the beds so that they each rested on the floor. This left them very little room, given that the desk was typically loaded with papers and trash. The entire suite was always messy. Zuckerberg had a habit of leaving food wrappers and empty cans and bottles all over the place. "He'd finish a beer or a Red Bull, put it down, and there it would stay for weeks,"[29] Kirkpatrick notes. Sometimes Moskovitz's girlfriend got tired of the clutter and threw out the trash. Once, when Zuckerberg's mother was visiting, she apologized to Moskovitz for her son's untidiness. "When he was growing up he had a nanny,"[30] she explained.

In the midst of this clutter was Zuckerberg's 8-foot-long whiteboard (2.4m), which he used for brainstorming ideas and writing out formulas. The only place it fit was along the wall in the hallway between the bedrooms. "He really loved that whiteboard," recalls Moskovitz. "He always wanted to draw out his ideas, even when that didn't necessarily make them clearer."[31] In contrast to his messiness, Zuckerberg's handwriting was painstakingly neat and tiny. He sometimes filled up entire notebooks with extensive reflections.

Multiple Projects

Zuckerberg was brimming with ideas for new Internet services. He spent many hours writing software code, often going without sleep and neglecting his homework in his non–computer science classes. On most nights he was found at his desk in the common room, hunched over his computer, exploring new ways to share information. He and his suitemates generally got along well, and they became involved with each other's projects.

Computer programming and the Internet were recurring topics of interest for the four young men. Zuckerberg and Moskovitz had ongoing friendly debates about website features and how the Internet might evolve as its number of users increased. Hughes, who initially had no interest in computers, became intrigued with the discussions and began sharing his opinions, as did Olson. Zuckerberg dreamed up new programming projects, and the other three men offered their suggestions on how to develop them. "I had like twelve projects that year," says Zuckerberg. "Of course I wasn't fully committed to any one of them." Most of them focused on "seeing how people were connected through mutual references."[32]

During the first week of his sophomore year, Zuckerberg created Course Match, a program that helped Harvard students choose classes, register online, and form study groups based on the course selections of other students. As Zuckerberg put

A Teacher's View of Mark Zuckerberg

Harvard University computer science professor Harry Lewis taught both Microsoft founder Bill Gates and Facebook creator Mark Zuckerberg. He maintains that Gates and Zuckerberg shared a similar approach to learning when they were college students:

> The thing I would say about Zuckerberg is that he was very eager to learn and very skeptical about whether anything we were teaching him was actually the right things for him to be learning. I think Bill Gates had exactly the same feeling. It was not disrespect for what was being taught, but maybe [it was] not exactly what he was interested in … so he was … absorbing everything and not paying any attention to it at the same time.

Quoted in CNBC. *Mark Zuckerberg: Inside Facebook.* Documentary. January 26, 2012.

it, the new program was a way of "link[ing] to people through things."[33] Course Match was instantly popular, and hundreds of students began using it. He ran the program from his dorm room laptop computer, and it eventually crashed because of the high demand. Later that school year, Zuckerberg created an online community study guide for his Art in the Time of Augustus course. Having barely attended the class all semester, he needed a way to cram for the final exam. He compiled a series of images from the course and e-mailed other class members, inviting them to contribute to the study guide by adding comments next to the images. After spending an evening reading their notes, he passed the exam.

Hot, Hotter, Hottest?

During that fall semester of 2003, however, the most notorious program Zuckerberg devised was the one that came together during the last week in October. It introduced Harvard to a rebellious, mischievous side of Zuckerberg. The purpose of the program, named Facemash, was to find out who was the most attractive person on campus. A user was invited to compare pictures of two students of the same gender and vote on which one was "hotter." As a student's rating went up, he or she would be compared to others who had been rated hotter, until the "hottest" was chosen.

Zuckerberg began creating the new program on Tuesday evening, October 28, after he had an argument with a young woman. In his blog, *Harvard Face Mash: The Process*, which he included along with the software, he insulted the girl and wrote, "I need to think of something to make to take my mind off her. I need to think of something to occupy my mind."[34]

Zuckerberg occupied himself by looking at student pictures in the Kirkland House facebook, a who's who book of people in his dorm similar to the book he had at Exeter. Each Harvard dorm maintained this kind of student directory, which listed the names of all its students alongside their photos. The photos were of poor quality, similar to the kind of pictures on driver's licenses,

Zuckerberg poses on the Harvard campus in 2004, months after he was nearly expelled for creating a notorious program called Facemash.

and were taken the day students arrived for orientation. "I'm a little intoxicated, not gonna lie. So what?" wrote Zuckerberg of his thought process that night. "The Kirkland facebook is open on my computer desktop and some of these people have pretty horrendous facebook pics."[35]

Through the rest of that night, Zuckerberg found ways to download the digital facebooks of nine of Harvard's twelve houses. A friend at Lowell House gave Zuckerberg temporary use of his password. At another dorm, Zuckerberg physically snuck in to download data from an ethernet cable he plugged into the wall. Most of the time he simply hacked in over the Internet and continued to blog about his adventure.

Zuckerberg's initial impulse was to compare each student to a picture of a farm animal. It was his suitemate Billy Olson who suggested comparing each person with another person and only occasionally including a farm animal. By the time most of the preliminary data had been downloaded—by 4:00 A.M., according to Zuckerberg's blog—the animal pictures had been dropped.

Launching Facemash

Zuckerberg took a few more days to write the algorithms—complex mathematical programs—to make the website work. When the site was nearly completed, Zuckerberg seemed to recognize that the project might get him in trouble. As he wrote in his blog, "Perhaps Harvard will squelch [Facemash] for legal reasons. ... But one thing is certain, and it's that I'm a jerk for making this site. Oh well. Someone had to do it eventually." Launching Facemash on the afternoon of Sunday, November 2, he included a terse introduction on its home page: "Were we let in [to Harvard] for our looks? No. Will we be judged by them? Yes."[36]

Zuckerberg e-mailed the link to his new site to a few friends, wanting to test it out. Those friends then forwarded the link to other friends, including those in other dorms and on various student e-mail lists. Traffic skyrocketed. Within a few hours the site had logged 450 visitors and 22,000 votes. Around 10:00 P.M., when Zuckerberg returned to his room after a meeting, Facemash was so flooded with users that he could not log on to his own computer.

The site was an immediate underground hit, but not everyone was happy with Zuckerberg's shenanigans. Complaints of sexism and racism spread among members of two campus women's groups—Fuerza Latina and the Association of Black Harvard Women. At about 10:30 P.M., Harvard's computer services department traced the source of Facemash to Zuckerberg's computer and shut off his web access.

Apologies and a Campus Hearing

The following day Zuckerberg e-mailed apology letters to Fuerza Latina and the Association of Black Harvard Women, explaining that he had only intended to conduct an experiment and get a few friends' opinions on it. "I wanted some more time to think about whether or not this was really appropriate to release to the Harvard community," he wrote. "This is not how I meant for things to go, and I apologize for any harm done as a result of my neglect to consider how quickly the site would spread and its consequences thereafter. ... I definitely see how my intentions could be seen in the wrong light." In a November 4, 2003, interview and article in the campus newspaper, Zuckerberg claimed he never expected to gain such widespread publicity and that he had decided to shut Facemash down for good: "The primary concern is hurting people's feelings. I'm not willing to risk insulting anyone."[37]

On November 18, 2003, Zuckerberg appeared before Harvard's disciplinary administrative board. Joining him at the hearing was his suitemate Billy Olson, who had contributed ideas to the Facemash project; the student who had given Zuckerberg the Lowell House password; and Harvard junior Joe Green, a dorm neighbor who had also helped out. Zuckerberg was charged with breach of security, copyright infringement, and violation of privacy. He apologized but also suggested that he had done Harvard a favor by revealing the security vulnerabilities of the sites he had so easily hacked. The deans were not pleased by this justification, but they decided not to expel Zuckerberg and placed him on probation instead.

After the hearing Zuckerberg celebrated his relatively light punishment by sharing a bottle of champagne with his Kirkland neighbors and seemed not to care much that he had narrowly averted big trouble. Green's father, a professor, was by chance visiting his son on the night of this celebration. "My dad was trying to drill it into Mark's head that this was really a big deal, that he'd almost gotten suspended," Green recalls. "But Mark didn't want to hear it. My dad came away with the notion that I shouldn't do any more Zuckerberg projects."[38]

Collaborations with Others

For others, however, the Facemash stunt was proof that Zuckerberg had a flair for making software that people loved to use, and many were eager to collaborate with him. Occasionally, he worked on other people's projects. Wanting to make up for the offense caused by Facemash, for example, he helped the Association of Black Harvard Women set up its own website.

In late November 2003 he was approached by three senior students—twins Cameron and Tyler Winklevoss and their friend Divya Narendra—who were building a student socializing website they called the Harvard Connection. The site would have two sections, "Dating" and "Connecting," where students could post pictures of themselves along with some personal information. Narendra and the Winklevoss twins had started constructing the Harvard Connection in December 2002, hiring some students to write code for it, but at the end of 2003 it remained unfinished. After reading about the Facemash episode in the campus newspaper, the three wanted Zuckerberg to do the programming for Harvard Connection. He agreed to help them out.

Harvard students Tyler Winklevoss, left, Divya Narendra, and Cameron Winklevoss approached Zuckerberg in November 2003 about writing code for a website called Harvard Connection.

According to Narendra and the Winklevoss brothers, Zuckerberg initially seemed excited about their project. On the day after their first meeting, Zuckerberg sent them an e-mail saying he would be able to set up Harvard Connection fairly quickly. Over the next two weeks, he spent about ten hours writing code for the "Connecting" section of the site. Then, as more weeks passed, Zuckerberg apparently lost interest in the project. Narendra and the Winklevosses contend that Zuckerberg promised to do more work but kept postponing meeting with them, claiming that his schedule was keeping him too busy.

A New Project

Part of what was keeping Zuckerberg busy was a project of his own that he started during the winter break. According to Zuckerberg, this new project was largely inspired by editorials about Facemash in the *Harvard Crimson*, the campus newspaper. One editorial suggested that "some [students] might wish to have their picture and personal information available to only a portion of the community ... a request that is easy enough to accommodate with reasonable coding."[39] Other *Crimson* articles expressed a popular sentiment among Harvard students at the time: that the university should take the photo directories—the facebooks—maintained by each house, combine them, and make them available online in searchable form.

Students at other colleges were pushing for the same thing. New interactive services, such as Friendster and MySpace, had recently sprouted up on the Internet. Students were eager to see campus-focused websites where they could search for others according to their interests and create an online network of friends.

Encouraged by the Harvard community's desire for an online directory, Zuckerberg combined elements from two of his previous projects—Course Match and Facemash—with ideas borrowed from Friendster. The result was a new website, founded on January 11, 2004, when Zuckerberg officially registered a web address as thefacebook.com. TheFacebook was to serve as an online communications tool and directory that would enable students to share information and keep track of their classmates. While Friendster was seen mainly as a dating site, Zuckerberg initially saw TheFacebook "as a tool to strengthen a network that already exists,"[40] according to an article in the *Crimson*.

In the meantime the creators of the Harvard Connection were still waiting to hear about Zuckerberg's progress on their website. Cameron Winklevoss e-mailed Zuckerberg on January 6: "hey mark, drop me a line when you get a chance."[41] Zuckerberg apologized by e-mail two days later, again claiming that he was swamped with homework and programming projects. Finally, he met with Narendra and the Winklevosses on January 14, telling them that they needed to find another programmer for their site.

TheFacebook Is Born

On that day, the three Harvard Connection partners had no idea that Zuckerberg had officially registered a website that was to serve as an online network for the university. Nor did they know that on January 12, Zuckerberg had contacted his fraternity brother, a business-savvy junior named Eduardo Saverin, to discuss marketing strategies for TheFacebook. After his experiences with Course Match and Facemash—which both had caused his computer to crash—Zuckerberg knew he needed to find a larger server to host TheFacebook. Moreover, since he had gotten in trouble with Harvard's administration board over Facemash, he wanted a server that was not affiliated with Harvard. With the help of a hosting site, he found a suitable place to store TheFacebook's software and data. Zuckerberg and Saverin each invested one thousand dollars to help pay the monthly fees for the server. Saverin was given ownership of 30 percent of TheFacebook in exchange for his investment and business advice.

On February 4 TheFacebook went live. In an article in the *Harvard Crimson*, Zuckerberg admitted that he had worn himself out getting the network started: "If I hadn't launched it that day, I was about to just can it and go on to the next thing."[42] His hard work bore fruit. The first users of TheFacebook, Zuckerberg's Kirkland neighbors, sent e-mails to other students asking them to join. This led to yet more invitations to an increasing number of friends, with dozens signing up right away. By the fifth day after launch, about one thousand students had joined, and TheFacebook had become a main topic of conversation at meals and between classes.

Part of the appeal of TheFacebook was its exclusivity and its privacy controls. Only people with a Harvard e-mail address could sign up, and profiles included a single photo with a user's

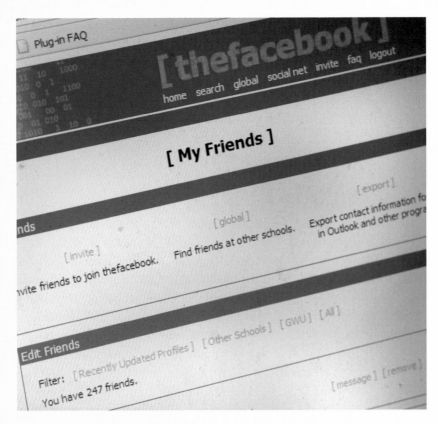

A screenshot shows the early design of TheFacebook, which went live in February 2004. Within three weeks, over six thousand users had joined the site.

real name along with other personal information the user was willing to share. Users were also able to set their privacy options to limit who could see their information—perhaps just current students, or only people in their own dormitory. Zuckerberg had a personal reason for creating these features. As a *Crimson* article pointed out, he "hoped the privacy options would help to restore his reputation following student outrage over facemash.com."[43] These features also distinguished TheFacebook from other social networks, such as Friendster and MySpace.

By the end of its first three weeks, TheFacebook had more than six thousand users. Zuckerberg, realizing that he needed more help to operate the website, enlisted his suitemates. He hired Dustin Moskovitz as vice president of programming, while Chris Hughes became director of publicity. The team's first priority, Zuckerberg insisted, would be to add more colleges to the network. He brought in California Institute of Technology student Adam D'Angelo, his inventing buddy from high school, to help set up databases at other universities.

A Stolen Idea?

The emergence of TheFacebook deeply angered the Harvard Connection partners. They claimed that Zuckerberg stole their idea and intentionally postponed work on their site so he could launch his site first. In an interview with the *Crimson*, Cameron Winklevoss said that Zuckerberg "boasted about completing [TheFacebook] in a week, after leading us on for three months. We passed through Thanksgiving, winter break and intercession. He had ample time. He not only led us on, but he knew what he was doing."[44] Zuckerberg firmly disputed this charge, pointing out that the idea of a social network was simply a sign of the times: "There aren't very many new ideas floating around," he told the *Crimson*. "The facebook isn't even a very novel idea. It's taken from all these others. And ours was that we're going to do it on the level of schools."[45]

Evidence reveals, however, that the Harvard Connection partners were correct about Zuckerberg leading them on. In an instant message sent in early January 2004, Zuckerberg told his friend Saverin to check out HarvardConnection.com and wrote: "They made a mistake haha. They asked me to make it for them. So I'm like delaying it so it won't be ready until after the facebook thing comes out."[46]

The Winklevosses sent a formal letter to Zuckerberg, demanding that he shut down TheFacebook or else they would charge him with breaking the school's honor code. They also met directly with Harvard president Lawrence Summers, hoping to persuade him to take action against Zuckerberg. In response Zuckerberg sent his own letter to Harvard administrators—and

A college student spends time exploring TheFacebook. The Harvard Connection partners were quick to accuse Zuckerberg of stealing their idea, first appealing to the university for action against him before filing a lawsuit.

a copy to the Winklevosses—defending himself: "Frankly, I'm kind of appalled that they're threatening me after the work I've done for them free of charge." He added: "I try to shrug it off as a minor annoyance that whenever I do something successful, every capitalist out there wants a piece of the action."[47] After reading both the Winklevosses' complaint and Zuckerberg's response, Summers decided that the matter was beyond the university's jurisdiction and suggested that the Harvard Connection team seek legal advice.

By the end of March 2004, TheFacebook had expanded to several other universities, including Columbia, Stanford, Yale, Princeton, Brown, and the Massachusetts Institute of Technology. The number of active users surpassed thirty thousand. On April 13 Saverin officially made TheFacebook a business by setting it up as a limited liability company (LLC) in Florida, his state of residence. Saverin became chief financial officer of the company. Zuckerberg irreverently posted his own job description as: "Founder, Master and Commander, [and] Enemy of the State."[48] What he wrote was, in part, a joke—but it also bespoke the confidence, verve, and determination that he would exhibit in the months to come.

Chapter 3

Building a Social Network

The months of March and April 2004 marked a turning point for Mark Zuckerberg and his popular new social network. At California's Stanford University, 85 percent of the student population joined TheFacebook within twenty-four hours of its launch at the university. After Stanford, each time the website became available at another college, almost all students signed up for it. Zuckerberg and his team received an increasing number of e-mails from around the United States urging them to offer TheFacebook at other schools. Its spread, however, was initially limited by server capacities. TheFacebook team was still renting power, paying $450 a month for five servers. Zuckerberg and Dustin Moskovitz constantly had to program and reconstruct the website so that it could take on new users—all while carrying a full load of classes at Harvard.

To keep up with the growing costs of running TheFacebook, Eduardo Saverin sought out advertisers and investors. Zuckerberg was initially reluctant to include ads on the website, but Saverin convinced him of their need for revenue. Zuckerberg placed certain limits on advertisers, however. He turned down offers from companies that did not seem to reflect TheFacebook's lighthearted attitude. He also restricted the size of the advertisers' displays and included captions above them that stated: "We don't like these either but they pay the bills."[49]

For Zuckerberg, money was not a priority. He claimed that his goal in life was "not to have a job. ... Making cool things is just something I love doing." However, he also admitted, "I assume eventually I'll make something that is profitable."[50] As Zuckerberg added new functions to TheFacebook, investors emerged to support his project, and new members joined in droves.

Meeting Sean Parker

One well-known developer from California's Silicon Valley, Sean Parker, heard about TheFacebook when it became a hit on the Stanford campus. Parker had helped to build Napster, an online music file-sharing service, and cofounded Plaxo, an online address book and network. Excited about TheFacebook's potential, Parker e-mailed Zuckerberg and offered to connect him with investors in San Francisco.

Parker flew to New York City in early April 2004, where he met Saverin, Zuckerberg, and their girlfriends for dinner at a fashionable Chinese restaurant. Zuckerberg, enthusiastic about the kinds of innovations Napster had accomplished, was delighted to meet Parker. Likewise, Parker was impressed with Zuckerberg's brilliance and ambition. The two fell into an intense dialogue about what TheFacebook might become. As Parker recalls, Zuckerberg "was not thinking, 'Let's make some money and get out.' This wasn't like a get-rich-quick scheme. This was 'Let's build something that has lasting cultural value and try to take over the world.' But he didn't know what that meant. Taking over the world meant taking over college."[51]

By the end of May 2004, TheFacebook did appear to be taking over prestigious colleges, with a user population up to 150,000 at thirty-four campuses just four months after its launch. The advertising firm Y2M tried to convince TheFacebook team to expand to even larger universities, but Zuckerberg insisted that membership remain limited to students, staff, and graduates of Ivy League and other elite schools. TheFacebook took up much of Zuckerberg's free time, but he still thought of it as just one of his several projects. In the meantime he delved into

Napster founder Sean Parker first shared his vision for TheFacebook with Zuckerberg in the spring of 2004. He went on to become the company's president.

yet another new venture. With Harvard sophomore Andrew McCollum, he began developing software that would allow its users to exchange any kind of digital information, including music, video, photos, and text files. They named it Wirehog, and it would lead to new features and applications on a later version of Facebook.

Moving to Silicon Valley

McCollum had a summer 2004 internship at a video game company near Palo Alto, California. This Northern California city is within the region known as Silicon Valley, home to many of the world's largest technology corporations. Zuckerberg decided that the summer would be a good time to explore this area, particularly with McCollum being there and with his Exeter friend Adam D'Angelo willing to join them. He used Craigslist to find a Silicon Valley house to rent for the summer. He recruited Moskovitz and two interns to join him and the others. Using fifteen thousand dollars of capital secured by Saverin, they all moved to a home at 819 La Jennifer Way in Palo Alto. Saverin decided not to go, electing to seek out more advertisers in New York instead.

One day in early June 2004, Zuckerberg and his companions were carrying groceries back to their rented house in Palo Alto and by chance ran into Sean Parker, the Internet developer Zuckerberg had met in New York two months earlier. Parker's

Silicon Valley

The phrase "Silicon Valley" first appeared in January 1971 as part of a series of articles published in the weekly trade newspaper *Electronic News*. Journalist Don Hoefler coined the phrase to describe the high number of companies in the semiconductor and computer industries that had emerged around the southern part of San Francisco Bay in California. Earlier in the twentieth century, this region was also known for its innovators in the electronics industry, with Stanford University graduates and the U.S. Navy producing new radio, television, and military technologies. Encompassing the cities of Palo Alto, San Jose, and South San Francisco, Silicon Valley is home to thousands of high-tech companies, including Apple, eBay, Google, Yahoo, Hewlett-Packard, and Facebook.

girlfriend happened to live just down the street from the house on La Jennifer Way. Upon hearing that Parker had lost about half of his shares in an Internet company he had cofounded, Zuckerberg invited him to move into the house with the rest of TheFacebook team. Parker accepted, taking a room furnished with one bare mattress. He agreed to share his BMW with Zuckerberg and the other housemates. For a time it was their only car.

Avoiding Technical Difficulties

TheFacebook team's summer work consisted mostly of refining and shoring up the site for the upcoming semester. The website experienced a drop in traffic during the summer, when most college students were away from school, but Zuckerberg expected growth to pick up again in the fall. At the same time, Zuckerberg was not certain that TheFacebook would experience continued success. As Parker recounts, "He had these doubts. Was it a fad?

In the early days of TheFacebook, Zuckerberg and his team were careful to avoid the fate of Friendster, another social networking site that experienced frequent service outages after expanding too quickly.

Was it going to go away? He liked the idea of TheFacebook, and he was willing to pursue it doggedly, tenaciously, to the end. But like the best empire builders, he was both very determined and very skeptical."[52]

One of Zuckerberg's main concerns was keeping TheFacebook free of technical glitches. An online network could easily fail if it expanded too quickly and experienced service outages. This is what had happened to Friendster—it grew too fast and became too clogged with users, causing the site to slow down and freeze up. This is one of the reasons that it eventually failed as a social network.

To avoid being "Friendstered," Zuckerberg and his team continually upgraded the database and reconfigured the servers in a way that enabled TheFacebook to hold ten times more users that it had at the moment. In addition, Zuckerberg and Moskovitz carefully paced TheFacebook's growth. They would launch the website at a new campus, observe the initial surge in membership, and allow the traffic to slow down and level off. If they experienced technical difficulties or did not yet have the money to buy more server power, they would wait before adding another school. Thus, TheFacebook's expansion was methodical and deliberate. In Zuckerberg's words, "We didn't just go out and get a lot of investment and scale it. We kind of intentionally slowed it down at the beginning. We literally rolled it out school by school."[53]

The Daily Work Routine

The environment at the Palo Alto house was a quirky combination of dormitory, fraternity house, and computer lab. Zuckerberg and his team established a daily routine of sleeping late and then heading to the dining room table, which was crowded with computers, cables, modems—and bottles, cans, and food wrappers—to work. As they programmed, no one talked. All communication occurred through their computers by instant messaging, even if they were sitting right next to one another. This helped them concentrate. Writer David Kirkpatrick notes, "Geeks like Zuckerberg

Dustin Moscovitz, left, was one of several people who worked with Zuckerberg on building and rolling out TheFacebook in the summer and fall of 2004.

and Moskovitz like to get deep into what is almost a trance when they're coding, and while they don't mind background music or the TV playing, they couldn't stand interruptions."[54]

Zuckerberg typically wore a T-shirt and pajamas for work. He slept later than most of the others, usually starting work in the afternoon and continuing late into the night. Although the interns did most of the tedious work, Zuckerberg sometimes stayed up all night, if necessary, to keep the system running. He also spent a lot of time refining Wirehog and programming other features for TheFacebook. Interestingly, neither Zuckerberg nor his summer team were themselves big users of TheFacebook. As they gathered information about its users, though, they learned that some people spent a lot of time on the website, looking through dozens of profiles each day. The team aimed to structure the site for this kind of user.

Sometimes the team would raucously discuss and debate ideas. When this happened, Zuckerberg paced back and forth around the dining room. He had brought his fencing equipment with him, and he liked to grab his foil, lunge, and slice it through the air as he made his points. Moskovitz did not appreciate this. "I'm the personality type where that would get [to] me sometimes," he explains. "It was a pretty small room. I'm like a cautious mother—'You're going to break something!' But when he got into the mood he would do it for a couple of hours."[55] Eventually the team banned Zuckerberg's indoor fencing.

Horseplay and Partying

Zuckerberg and his friends did not spend all of their time working. Late at night they took breaks to drink beer, watch movies, and play video games. Parker was the only one in the group who was over twenty-one, so they relied on him to purchase alcohol. Sometimes he bought marijuana to share as well, but Zuckerberg would not smoke it.

The house had a pool in the backyard. McCollum strung a cable from the chimney on top of the house to a pole next to the pool, creating a zip line so that people could slide down from the roof and into the water. TheFacebook team liked to grill steaks and hang out poolside, drinking, swimming, and talking loudly late into the night. They sometimes used TheFacebook to announce house parties, attracting local youths and mobs of students from nearby Stanford University. Some people came over and hung out for several days.

The parties frequently included drinking games such as beer pong, in which opposing teams throw a Ping-Pong ball into cups of beer arranged at one end of a table. If a ball ends up in an opponent's cup, the loser must drink its contents. Drunken shenanigans led to broken furniture, broken bottles, and broken doors. Trash, barbecue ashes, and shards of glass often ended up in the pool, and neighbors complained about the late-night rowdiness.

Company Conflicts

Despite all the boisterous partying, TheFacebook was becoming a serious enterprise. Zuckerberg turned down a financier's $10 million dollar offer for TheFacebook in June 2004. With chief financial officer Saverin in New York drumming up advertisers, Zuckerberg began to rely more on Parker for advice on securing assets and expanding the business. Parker had experience in developing Internet companies, as well as connections with investors. Parker also recognized that TheFacebook's LLC status would not be sufficient for a growing business, and he convened with a lawyer to restructure the fledgling company.

With school out for the summer, TheFacebook's advertising sales slowed down. Zuckerberg needed money to buy new equipment and began using some of his own savings as well as contributions from his parents. In mid-June Parker started meeting with investors about financing TheFacebook. Saverin became upset when he heard about this. He wrote a letter to Zuckerberg, arguing that the original agreement among the partners gave him control over TheFacebook's business strategies. He now demanded a contract to guarantee him that control.

Thus began a deep disagreement between Zuckerberg and Saverin. In Zuckerberg's opinion Saverin was demanding to be chief executive officer (CEO) of TheFacebook without making a full-time commitment, as the other partners had. Moreover, as Zuckerberg explained in a legal filing, "until [Saverin] had written authority to do what he wanted with the business, he would obstruct ... the advancement of the business itself. ... Since he owned 30 percent ... he would make it impossible for the business to raise any financing until this matter was resolved."[56] For example, at one crucial moment, when Zuckerberg needed to purchase new servers, Saverin froze TheFacebook's bank account, refusing to release any money until his demands were met. That action required Zuckerberg and his parents to spend eighty-five thousand dollars of their own funds to keep TheFacebook running.

Saverin's demands were not entirely unreasonable. Early on he had invested thousands of dollars in TheFacebook, and he

Eduardo Saverin, TheFacebook's first chief financial officer, became upset when Sean Parker began courting investors without Saverin's consent. This rift ultimately led to Saverin being fired from the company.

had been meeting with advertisers to bring in revenue. This was often difficult work, and it was made more frustrating because Zuckerberg was nonchalant about revenue and preferred to keep ads to a minimum. As the two friends argued by phone and letter about their roles and responsibilities, Parker completed the legal negotiations that restructured TheFacebook as a corporation. Saverin retained some ownership, but was eventually fired from the company. The new bylaws made Zuckerberg TheFacebook's sole director, with Parker as the company president.

Seed Money

Along with negotiating TheFacebook's corporate status, Parker arranged for Zuckerberg to meet Peter Thiel, a cofounder of PayPal and a professional investor. Impressed with how quickly students were joining TheFacebook as soon as it became available at their campus, Thiel agreed to a loan of five hundred thousand dollars.

It was just what TheFacebook needed. By the beginning of the fall semester of 2004, membership had increased to two hundred thousand. Zuckerberg and his team needed to buy new servers to accommodate the growing demand. During the first week of the new semester, they added fifteen new colleges, and TheFacebook began to expand to larger universities and non–Ivy League schools.

Anticipating a very busy year for TheFacebook, Zuckerberg decided not to return to Harvard. Moskovitz and McCollum also elected to stay in Silicon Valley. Since they had to vacate the Palo Alto house, the remaining members of TheFacebook team moved to a new rental in Los Altos Hills. There would be no more complaints from neighbors about late-night rowdiness—this house, dubbed Casa Facebook, was right next to a busy interstate with traffic noise that blocked out other sounds.

PayPal cofounder Peter Thiel invested five hundred thousand dollars in TheFacebook in 2004, which allowed the company to purchase the new servers it needed to accommodate its ever-growing number of members.

New Features and Accelerating Growth

In September 2004 Zuckerberg introduced two new elements to TheFacebook. One, the Wall, allowed members to write comments and messages directly on other members' profiles. The comments would be visible to anyone who read a user's profile, and others could write responses to those comments in their own posts to the Wall. The other addition, Groups, allowed a user to create a group based on any interest or topic. A Group could have its own page—similar to an individual's profile—complete with its own Wall where comments could be posted.

The Wall was especially popular. With the data they had gathered over the summer, TheFacebook team knew that people spent hours just looking through profiles on the website. Because it offered more information on members, the Wall increased this tendency for people to log in and linger on TheFacebook, wandering from profile to profile.

TheFacebook's membership grew rapidly. By the end of September 2004, it reached four hundred thousand—nearly doubling in one month. It got up to half a million members on October 21, then skyrocketed to 1 million members by November 30. By mid-February 2005 TheFacebook had 2 million active members at 370 colleges. Sixty-five percent of them were logging on daily, and 90 percent were returning to the site at least once a week. This phenomenal growth—from a handful of friends to 2 million members—occurred just one year after TheFacebook's dorm-room launch.

A Moral Dilemma

As TheFacebook grew and expanded, it attracted more interest from investors. Twelve venture capital firms and four high-tech companies, including Sequoia Capital and Viacom, owner of MTV, made huge money offers. Zuckerberg turned them down. He wanted to be careful about taking on investors, because they could make demands that would leave him with less control over the site. But early in 2005 Zuckerberg and his team met with Donald Graham, CEO of the Washington Post Company. They entered into negotiations in which the company would invest $6 million in TheFacebook in return for 10 percent company ownership. In an unofficial agreement made over the phone, Graham told Zuckerberg that the Washington Post Company would invest without demanding a seat on TheFacebook's board of directors. This meant that Zuckerberg would have funding while retaining control of the site.

There was one complication. Accel Partners, a venture capital firm, had also entered into investment negotiations with TheFacebook. At a dinner meeting in Palo Alto, Accel offered

$12.7 million for 11 percent of the company—doubling the offer that Graham had made. Zuckerberg, quiet and pensive, excused himself to go to the bathroom. He was gone for a long time—such a long time that Matt Cohler, a recent recruit of TheFacebook team who was also at the dinner, went to look for him. He found Zuckerberg in the men's room, sitting cross-legged on the floor with his head down. Zuckerberg was crying. "Through his tears he was saying, 'This is wrong. I can't do this. I gave my word!'"[57] Cohler recalls. Zuckerberg preferred the investment deal with Accel, but had already unofficially agreed to the offer from Graham. Cohler advised Zuckerberg simply to telephone Graham and ask his opinion.

From TheFacebook to Facebook

September 20, 2005, marked another milestone for Mark Zuckerberg and his growing social network. TheFacebook dropped the "The" from its title and officially became Facebook. Sean Parker, who had always felt the use of "The" was awkward, negotiated for

TheFacebook changed its name to simply Facebook in 2005.

weeks with AboutFace, the business that first used the web address Facebook.com to sell software for company personnel directories. While AboutFace was not interested in TheFacebook's offer of stock as payment, it did accept Parker's payment of two hundred thousand dollars in cash. This was Parker's last significant move as president of the company.

The following day Zuckerberg called Graham, explaining what had happened and admitting that he was in a moral dilemma. Graham's response was gracious. He acknowledged that he did not have the resources that Accel had to offer and released Zuckerberg from the investment deal with the Washington Post Company. Zuckerberg went on to finalize the negotiations with Accel. He also—partly because of what he had learned through his business discussions with Graham—sealed the deal in a way that left him with most of the control over TheFacebook.

May 26, 2005, the day Zuckerberg signed the papers with Accel, ended somewhat disturbingly. Now a millionaire, Zuckerberg wanted to have a quiet, low-key celebration. Heading out on a late night drive to visit his girlfriend across town, Zuckerberg stopped at a gas station in a poor neighborhood in East Palo Alto. As he was filling his tank, a very intoxicated man approached him with a gun, demanding money. Zuckerberg was terrified, but he took a chance. He jumped into his car and drove away. In reflecting on his escape, Zuckerberg said, "I'm just lucky to be alive."[58] The growth of TheFacebook might be described similarly—as a surprisingly successful venture emerging from an unpredictable combination of smarts, luck, and risk taking.

Chapter 4

Triumph and Controversy

By the fall of 2005, Mark Zuckerberg's nearly two-year-old social network had 5 million members. Eighty-five percent of college students in the United States had Facebook accounts. Sixty percent of them logged in daily. About twenty thousand new users were joining each day. Zuckerberg and his partners began to consider ways to open the network to more populations.

Turning a Dream into Reality

Zuckerberg had a broad vision for Facebook. His dream was for the network to become a vast communications system—a utility—similar to the way the telephone network had become a utility enabling people to connect with others over great distances. For this to happen, company advisors thought that Facebook needed to project a more serious image. It had to grow out of its reputation as a trendy college website run by rambunctious, party-throwing geeks. Such a transformation would not be easy. As Facebook expanded and matured, Zuckerberg made mistakes, faced setbacks and controversies, and found his personal and business reputation challenged in the media.

Zuckerberg's first significant challenge with the newly named Facebook was dealing with Sean Parker, the company president. Parker was savvy about starting new Internet companies, had a lot of connections in Silicon Valley, and had become a friend and trusted advisor. Yet Parker also had a reputation for partying, rebelliousness,

Zuckerberg gives an address at a technical conference in 2010. His original vision for Facebook was to create a vast communication network that could connect people all over the world.

and unpredictability. During a party he hosted in the late summer of 2005 while vacationing in North Carolina, for example, Parker was arrested—though not formally charged—for possession of cocaine. He was quickly released and allowed to return to California.

Zuckerberg initially decided not to take any action in the wake of Parker's arrest. Since Parker had not been officially charged with a crime, Zuckerberg was not convinced any wrongdoing had occurred. However, board member Jim Breyer was very concerned when he learned about the incident. Breyer was the representative for Accel, the venture firm that had invested $12.7 million in Facebook. He knew about allegations of Parker's drug use and recklessness at his previous places of work. Also, rumor had it that an underage female employee was at the party when Parker was arrested. Breyer did not feel this was appropriate behavior for a president of Facebook. He insisted that Parker resign and threatened to file a lawsuit for not being immediately informed about Parker's arrest. After two days of arbitration and emotional discussions between Zuckerberg and Parker, Parker agreed to step down.

Facebook's Next Steps

During the fall of 2005, Zuckerberg started allowing high school students to become members of Facebook. Some of the other Facebook executives disagreed with this idea at first, arguing that

A Facebook user checks out a photo shared by another user. When the ability to share photos was added to Facebook in 2006, it quickly became the site's most popular feature.

the college membership would not want younger people coming into a network originally established for adults. If Facebook was to become a communications utility, however, it needed to compete with MySpace, a large and growing social network that had become very popular with youths. As Breyer explained, "We knew that if we were going to win big, we had to start getting the hearts and minds of high schoolers."[59]

Facebook began allowing in younger students by encouraging its college members to invite their friends who were still in high school. At first, high school members were limited to a separate Facebook, where they could not see the profiles of college members. In February 2006 the two Facebooks were merged, allowing members to connect with other users regardless of their age or grade, with the minimum age for membership set at thirteen. By April 2006 over 1 million high school students had joined Facebook.

Other innovations continued to attract more members to Facebook. For example, Zuckerberg noticed that a lot of users enjoyed changing their profile photo—sometimes several times a day. Facebook's design at the time allowed just one photo per profile. So Zuckerberg enlisted his programmers to turn Facebook into a site where members could upload, share, and store multiple photos. In addition, members could identify, or tag, themselves and their friends in the photos. Photo sharing quickly became Facebook's most popular feature. Many members set up their profiles to receive e-mail alerts when they were tagged in photos, and these alerts encouraged them to return to Facebook more often. Within a month of launching the photo hosting feature, 85 percent of Facebook members had been tagged in photos, and 70 percent were logging in to the website daily.

New Elements Spark Protest

Zuckerberg and his team introduced two more Facebook features, the News Feed and Mini-Feed, on September 5, 2006. The News Feed appeared on every user's home page, showing all the Facebook activities (posts, comments, added photos) of all the friends in one's network, while the Mini-Feed recorded one's activities on one's own Wall. These elements allowed members to easily track their friends' Facebook movements by the minute. No longer would people have to click on individual profiles, or wander from one profile page to another, to see what their friends had posted. All updates were available on one's home page.

Complaints emerged immediately among Facebook's members. Many people felt that the News Feed edged too closely to violating privacy. Northwestern University student Ben Parr started a new group, Students Against Facebook News Feed, contending that "very few of us want everyone automatically knowing what we update. ... [The] news feed is just too creepy, too stalkeresque, and a feature that has to go."[60] Within a few days 750,000 members joined Students Against Facebook News Feed. Some of them called for sit-in protests at Facebook's headquarters in Palo Alto, and television news teams began gathering outside the offices. While demonstrations never materialized, the company hired security guards to help calm the nerves of frightened employees.

A Facebook user reviews her News Feed to track the statuses of her friends. The News Feed feature was controversial when it was first introduced in 2006, as some users expressed privacy concerns.

Zuckerberg was in New York on a business trip when this controversy erupted. Hoping to calm tensions by appealing to logic, he wrote a blog post clarifying that the News Feed had built-in protections: "None of your information is visible to anyone who couldn't see it in the first place."[61] This explanation did not satisfy Students Against Facebook News Feed, and it implied a lack of foresight and understanding on Zuckerberg's part. For one thing, the abrupt debut of a highly efficient feature caught many people off-guard. Even though information was shared only within one's network, users felt suddenly exposed, as if their updates were being broadcast publicly. While many people enjoyed sharing news and opinions with *some* friends in their network, they did not necessarily want *all* their friends to have quick access to everything they posted.

"We Really Messed This One Up"

In the end Zuckerberg admitted that he and his team had erred: "We really messed this one up," he wrote to members in a follow-up post. "We did a bad job of explaining what the new features were and an even worse job of giving you control over them. … We didn't build in the proper privacy controls right away. This was a big mistake on our part, and I'm sorry for it."[62] Facebook's engineers quickly revamped the News Feed, allowing users more control over what activities were displayed to their network. The uproar against the News Feed did not totally disappear, but it quieted down significantly.

Interestingly, as angry as some people were about the News Feed, the anti-Feed protest had grown so fast because users heard about it through their own News Feeds. Members who claimed to hate the feature still used it, and people began spending even more time on Facebook than they had prior to the addition of the News Feed. Zuckerberg had the figures to prove this: In August 2006, members viewed 12 billion pages through Facebook. By October, after the addition of the News Feed, they viewed 22 billion pages.

The autumn of 2006 marked another important milestone for Facebook. On September 26 the network became open to anyone age thirteen and over with a valid e-mail address. Facebook was no longer a student-focused system, and new members—fifty thousand or more a day—began pouring in.

Facebook's Headquarters

The Facebook office, located at 1 Hacker Way in Menlo Park, California, is housed in a spacious, large-windowed building on a 57-acre campus (23ha). Employees were consulted on what kinds of interior design would make their workday more creative and productive. This led to the formation of indoor neighborhoods that give each department a unique flavor. More than two thousand employees work in open spaces, rather than in separate, walled-off cubicles.

Workers at Facebook's headquarters enjoy a spacious open floor plan as well as meals, laundry service, and other perks.

The company provides three free meals a day, with snacks and beverages offered in mini-kitchens located throughout the building. Free laundry, board games, exercise areas, and relaxation lounges are also provided. Employees are encouraged to write on the walls, contribute artwork, and move furniture where they please. They can also bicycle and skateboard through the concrete-floored halls.

Decisions on Big Offers

Facebook's rapid growth continued to attract offers from investors and major companies. Yahoo offered Zuckerberg $1 billion to purchase Facebook. Michael Wolf, president of MTV, offered $1.5 billion. Microsoft upped the ante even more, offering $15 billion—a purchase that would have made over $4 billion for Zuckerberg personally. Feeling confident after the upsurge in

Facebook membership, Zuckerberg turned them all down. He still had a vision for the growing network and was less interested in accruing wealth than in nurturing and molding a technically based social tool to make the world more open and connected. As Zuckerberg mentioned in a company mission statement: "We don't build services to make money; we make money to build better services. ... These days I think more and more people want to use services from companies that believe in something beyond simply maximizing profits."[63]

Some board members and employees—about 150 total at the time—worried about Zuckerberg's decisions not to sell. He admitted these choices were not always easy for him to make, given that he was still quite young and "sort of learning on the job."[64] In a televised interview Zuckerberg said, "The hardest [decision] was really when Yahoo offered us a billion dollars, because that was the first really big offer, and ... at the time I knew nothing about business. I knew nothing about what a company could be worth, and I had to make this argument to people that somehow this was going to be the right decision."[65] Not everyone was persuaded, and some employees left the company. But most, including Zuckerberg's older sister, Randi, who had become Facebook's marketing director, stayed.

In October 2007 Microsoft came back to Facebook with a different kind of offer: an investment of $240 million in return for only 1.6 percent of the company. Zuckerberg accepted this deal, which set Facebook's value at $15 billion. The agreement allowed Microsoft to serve as a broker for ads that were to run on Facebook's U.S. site until 2011.

Facebook as an Ecosystem

Part of what had prompted Microsoft's investment was Zuckerberg's decision to launch Facebook Platform, a systemic feature that enabled outside parties to create programs that work on Facebook. In other words, the website was reconfigured into a platform for applications, commonly referred to as "apps". Facebook would serve as a supportive environment in which any programmer could build and share tools. Within weeks of

The Facebook Platform, launched in 2007, enabled the creation of games such as the popular FarmVille as well as other features.

the May 2007 launch of Facebook Platform, many new apps were built, providing numerous tools that allowed members to personalize their profiles with links, images, music, and videos. A variety of popular social games, such as FarmVille and Mafia Wars, emerged as well. These new features attracted millions of new members.

Back in 2004 Zuckerberg had created his own file-sharing program, Wirehog, but he had suspended it in 2006. By turning Facebook into a platform, Zuckerberg took the pressure off himself and his employees to create all the best new apps. As Zuckerberg explained at a conference in San Francisco:

> Companies like Microsoft or Google have tens of thousands of engineers. We're tiny compared to that. So … how can we ever possibly build all the stuff that we want to see out there? The answer is to build an ecosystem and make it so that all these developers—whether it's a student in a dorm room who hasn't had a job yet, a big company, or a company

that we've never heard of in some other country—can just build the stuff. And that's the part that's so cool about it.[66]

While their approaches differed from that of Facebook's, software giants Microsoft and Apple had also become successful by establishing their products as platforms. As it became obvious that millions were joining Facebook after its platform launch, Microsoft saw that the network was a good investment opportunity. In turn Microsoft's investment was an enormous boost to Facebook, which had 50 million active members by October 2007. It gave Zuckerberg the resources to hire hundreds more employees, buy technology to keep up with accelerating growth, and expand internationally. Undoubtedly, Zuckerberg was developing entrepreneurial skills.

A Major Misstep

Zuckerberg immediately launched more Facebook features after the Microsoft investment. On November 6, 2007, he hosted a gala for the New York advertising community, announcing that any commercial entity could create its own page on Facebook for free. A user could become a "fan" of these pages. When a member clicked the "become a fan" button on a page, it would be announced in their friends' News Feeds. It was a form of free advertising, but Zuckerberg also believed that it would encourage companies to purchase ad space once they saw the market possibilities. Facebook's online advertising potential was—and is—enormous, in part because it gathers information about its members. Details such as age, gender, musical tastes, hobbies, and so on can be used to place highly targeted ads.

Zuckerberg also introduced Beacon, a program that sent information about a member's purchases to their friends and to Facebook partner sites. It did this by tracking users' web-surfing habits, even when they were not logged in to Facebook. It also allowed Facebook's advertising partners to notify a user's friends when the user bought one of their products.

Beacon was a near disaster. Many members felt Facebook was invading their privacy to reap profits. Stories appeared in the press about people who had unintentionally announced their purchases to their friends on Facebook. A number of users found their entire Christmas gift list had been broadcast in the News Feed. Beacon even began to damage sales among some e-retailers, as people became reluctant to buy products through the Internet out of fear that their personal information was no longer protected.

A Backlash

The backlash was immediate. Several activist groups, led by the liberal organization MoveOn, filed complaints with the Federal Trade Commission. Some groups initiated lawsuits. Facebook was heavily criticized in the news media, and the damage to its image was compounded because Zuckerberg remained silent about the controversy for three weeks. On December 4, 2007, a harsh editorial by Josh Quittner appeared in *Fortune* magazine. He wrote: "Facebook has turned all the people who rooted for it into a lynch mob. In the space of a month, it's gone from media darling to devil. The most interesting thing about Facebook right now is who will replace it."[67]

On the following day Zuckerberg published an apologetic blog post. "We've made a lot of mistakes building this feature, but we've made even more with how we've handled them," he said. "We simply did a bad job with this release, and I apologize for it. ... We took too long to decide on the right solution."[68] Facebook users could turn Beacon off if they wished, and eventually the feature was dropped. This satisfied some of the protest groups that had filed complaints, but negative feelings about Facebook lingered. Membership growth slowed down noticeably that winter. It picked up again in 2008, but in the years to come, as Facebook's privacy policies were repeatedly overhauled, many members found themselves frustrated and confused about how much control they had over the information they shared online.

As a result of the Beacon fiasco, board member Breyer convinced Zuckerberg that Facebook needed a new chief operating officer (COO), someone experienced in public relations and online advertising. For this they recruited Sheryl Sandberg, formerly a

Former Google executive Sheryl Sandberg became Facebook's chief operating officer in 2008.

senior executive at Google. Zuckerberg remained CEO, but as COO Sandberg would now provide guidance in developing stable and effective business strategies.

Lawsuits Lead to Privacy Issues for Zuckerberg

Zuckerberg soon faced some embarrassing privacy issues of his own. Over the course of the lawsuits filed in September 2004 and in March 2008 by ConnectU creators Divya Narendra, Cameron Winklevoss, and Tyler Winklevoss, legal teams combed through Zuckerberg's computer, seeking evidence related to the case. They came across dozens of e-mails and instant messages sent by Zuckerberg while he was still a student at Harvard, many of which revealed him to be mean-spirited and unethical. Together, they painted a very unflattering picture of Facebook's CEO.

For example, in a January 2004 message to his friend Adam D'Angelo, Zuckerberg wrote, "I'm making that dating site. ... [It's] probably going to be released around the same time [as TheFacebook]. ... Unless I [screw] the dating site over and quit on them right before I told them I'd have it done."[69] In a later response to a question about what he was going to do about the two competing projects, Zuckerberg cursed and implied he would intentionally damage the other site's chances of success. In yet another leaked exchange, Zuckerberg told a friend, "if you ever need any info about anyone at harvard ... just ask ... i have over 4000 emails, pictures, addresses, sns [social security numbers]." When his friend asked why people had given him access to this data, Zuckerberg answered, "they 'trust me' ... dumb [idiots]."[70]

In a 2010 interview in the *New Yorker*, Zuckerberg stated that he "absolutely" regretted those instant messages. "If you're going to go on to build a service that is influential and that a lot of people rely on, then you need to be mature, right?" he said. "I think I've grown and learned a lot."[71] Zuckerberg's backers maintain he should not be judged by the antics he engaged in as a nineteen-year-old. One such supporter is Breyer, who said, "After having a great deal of time with Mark, my confidence in him as C.E.O.

Lawsuits Against Zuckerberg

Twin brothers Tyler and Cameron Winklevoss, along with classmate Divya Narendra, first contacted Zuckerberg in November 2003 to ask if he would program Harvard Connection (later renamed ConnectU), an online socializing site that they were developing for college students and planning to spread to other U.S. schools. Zuckerberg agreed but then lagged for months, claiming to be busy with schoolwork, before abandoning their project. They filed a lawsuit against Zuckerberg in September 2004, arguing that he stole their idea to build his own website. In 2008 Facebook settled the lawsuit for an estimated $65 million.

Cameron Winklevoss, left, and Tyler Winklevoss leave U.S. District Court in Boston, Massachusetts, in July 2007.

Eduardo Saverin, an early investor and partner, also sued Zuckerberg and TheFacebook, claiming he had been unethically ousted from the company in 2005. Facebook later settled the Saverin lawsuit for an undetermined amount and reinstated him in the company roster as a cofounder.

of Facebook [is] in no way shaken. He is a brilliant individual who, like all of us, has made mistakes."[72]

Zuckerberg on the Big Screen

Despite his mistakes, Zuckerberg had achieved phenomenal success by the end of 2010. In a mere six years, half a billion people had joined the website that he had first launched from his

Jesse Eisenberg, second from right, portrays Zuckerberg in a scene in which he and his friends create an early version of Facebook in their dorm room in the 2010 movie The Social Network.

computer in a messy dorm room. Facebook, with a continually changing mix of apps and features, was now the world's largest social network. At age twenty-six, Zuckerberg was the world's youngest billionaire. *Time* magazine named him Person of the Year for 2010, and *Vanity Fair* listed him as number one in that year's ranking of the New Establishment.

Zuckerberg's fame and wealth drew attention from the entertainment industry as well as the news media. In October 2010 *The Social Network*, a movie based on Zuckerberg's college years and the founding of Facebook, premiered. The screenplay, written by Aaron Sorkin, was drawn from Ben Mezrich's 2009 book, *The Accidental Billionaires*. Mezrich admitted that he had invented scenes based heavily on interviews with former friends who had fallen out with Zuckerberg. Like the book, the film portrayed Zuckerberg as socially inept, devious, spiteful, and envious, although he was not an entirely unsympathetic character.

Zuckerberg was crestfallen when he first learned about the movie. "I just wished that nobody made a movie of me while I was still alive,"[73] he said during an interview at a techie conference. He denied that his creation of Facebook was motivated by a need to prove himself to the cool crowd, as the film suggested. Later, in an appearance on *The Oprah Winfrey Show*, Zuckerberg said, "I can promise you, this is my life so I know it's not that dramatic. The last six years have been a lot of coding and focus and hard work, but maybe it would be fun to remember it as partying and all this crazy drama."[74] David Kirkpatrick, author of *The Facebook Effect*, maintains that the movie was only "40 percent true. ... [Zuckerberg] is not snide and sarcastic in a cruel way. ... A lot of the factual incidents are accurate, but many are distorted and the overall impression is false."[75] Nevertheless, *The Social Network* won a Golden Globe and an Academy Award.

Other media depictions were more lighthearted. Zuckerberg voiced himself in "Loan-a-Lisa," an October 2010 episode of the cartoon series *The Simpsons*, in which he tells Lisa Simpson that being successful does not require graduating from college. In January 2011 Zuckerberg made a surprise appearance on the comedy sketch show *Saturday Night Live*, which was being hosted by Jesse Eisenberg, the actor who played him in *The Social Network*. After calling Eisenberg his "evil twin" backstage, Zuckerberg walked onstage to join Eisenberg and Andy Samberg—a comic who often impersonates Zuckerberg on the show. When Eisenberg asked Zuckerberg what he thought of *The Social Network*, Zuckerberg chuckled and answered, "It was interesting."[76]

Difficult decisions, bold ideas, serious mistakes, personal embarrassments, and accelerating triumphs were all integral to Zuckerberg's first several years of learning on the job. As he continues to become seasoned as a leader in social media, Zuckerberg's ongoing challenge centers on how to sustain a growing worldwide communications network that promises openness as well as protects privacy.

Chapter 5

The Frugal Billionaire

By the beginning of 2012, Zuckerberg's dorm-room invention had become a seemingly unstoppable juggernaut in the world of social media. In spite of reports that Facebook had lost about 7 million users in North America during 2011, the network continued to grow, thanks to its adoption in multiple countries, including the large nations of India, Brazil, and Mexico. Its registered users number over 800 million. On February 1, 2012, Facebook filed for an initial public offering, the first step toward allowing the general public to buy shares in the company, which has been valued at nearly $100 billion. According to *Forbes* magazine, as of November 2011 Zuckerberg was the fourteenth richest American and the thirty-fifth richest person in the world. He was also the wealthiest person on the planet under the age of thirty.

Despite this extraordinary wealth, Zuckerberg lives a fairly modest life. In many ways Zuckerberg himself is a study in contrasts: a billionaire who lives frugally, a dropout who donates to educational causes, a hacker aiming to set new rules, and a private person who wants to make the world a more open place.

"I'm Just Like a Little Kid"

Zuckerberg has always maintained that having a great job and becoming rich were never priorities in his life. "I'm just like a little kid. I get bored easily and computers excite me," he mentioned

Zuckerberg and Priscilla Chan, left, met as students at Harvard University.

in an interview with the *Harvard Crimson*. "Making cool things is just something I love doing, and not having someone tell me what to do or a time frame in which to do it is the luxury I am looking for in my life."[77] He still prefers to wear gray T-shirts, jeans, flip-flops, and—in cool weather—fleece hoodies. According to Facebook COO Sheryl Sandberg, Zuckerberg typically buys multiple versions of the exact same shirts and jeans.

Zuckerberg, preferring cars that are "comfortable [and] not ostentatious,"[78] drives an Acura TSX, a low-end luxury sedan worth about thirty thousand dollars. Driving is one of the activities that helps him unwind, particularly after putting in twelve to sixteen hours at the office or on the computer. He also enjoys spending quality time with his wife, Priscilla Chan, whom he first met as a sophomore at Harvard. At one point, Chan, a medical student at the University of California–San Francisco, set strict rules for their relationship: "One date per week, a minimum of a hundred minutes of alone time, not in his apartment, and definitely not at Facebook."[79] They spend most weekends together—walking in the park, rowing (they get in separate boats and race), and playing bocce ball or board games. In September 2010 the two moved in together. In March 2011 they brought home a puppy—a fluffy, white-haired puli they named Beast. Not until then did they both change their Facebook profiles from "single" to "in a relationship." The two married on May 19, 2012.

Zuckerberg's living quarters have typically been Spartan. He has found all of his homes through Craigslist. One friend likened his first one-bedroom dwelling, furnished with a single futon, to a "crack den,"[80] although Zuckerberg does not use drugs. On September 24, 2010, Zuckerberg appeared on *The Oprah Winfrey Show* in an interview that included a peek into the modest four-bedroom Palo Alto house that he was then renting with Chan. Sparsely decorated, the rooms were painted in shades of blue and beige, except for the bright yellow kitchen. Zuckerberg is somewhat indifferent to colors. Through an online test, he discovered that he is red-green colorblind—which is why Facebook's primary color is blue.

In May 2011 Zuckerberg purchased a $7 million mansion in Palo Alto. The 5,600-square-foot abode (520 sq. m) includes a pool, an outdoor fireplace, and a master bathroom with twin marble-topped vanities, separate soaking tub, and heated floors. Although the house is luxurious by most Americans' standards, many media pundits were disappointed in what they perceived as an overly modest purchase for someone with Zuckerberg's wealth. As the *Daily Mail* pointed out, "Mr. Zuckerberg's home is still dwarfed by those of his Silicon Valley rivals."[81] The *Los Angeles Times* noted, "Even with this big purchase, Zuckerberg is still living below his means."[82] Gossip website TMZ quipped, "You paid $7 mil for that?"[83] Others maintained, however, that Zuckerberg was saving his fortune for more noble causes.

Charitable Activities

Zuckerberg's main reason for appearing on *Oprah* in 2010 was to announce his donation of $100 million to create the charitable foundation Startup: Education. Matched by a pledge from the

Zuckerberg, with Mayor Cory Booker in the background, discusses his $100 million donation to Startup: Education to benefit students in Newark, New Jersey, in 2010.

Newark Education and Youth Development Fund and Mayor Cory Booker of Newark, New Jersey, Zuckerberg's contribution is dedicated to improving the city's public school system. "I've had a lot of opportunities in my life, and a lot of that comes from having gone to really good schools,"[84] Zuckerberg told Winfrey. Although Zuckerberg has little connection to the city of Newark, he wrote in a blog post that "Newark has unfortunately become a symbol of public education's failure—of a status quo that accepts schools that don't succeed."[85]

Zuckerberg's motives for the donation were questioned. Because his appearance on *Oprah* occurred one week before the premiere of *The Social Network*, many pundits speculated the donation was a public-relations stunt designed to boost Facebook's image before movie audiences saw Zuckerberg portrayed in an unflattering light. *New York* magazine called it "the PR move of the month,"[86] while the *Wall Street Journal* quipped, "Mr. Zuckerberg may be young. But he already has learned a lot about the offsetting value of philanthropy."[87] However, Winfrey noted that Zuckerberg had initially intended to keep his donation anonymous. "You're such a shy person and you've been talking about this for months and months and months," she said to him on her show. "You wanted to remain anonymous and we talked you into coming on here."[88]

Journalists as well as colleagues have noted Zuckerberg's bashfulness, while others remark about his confidence. Some say that he exhibits both traits. Interviewer Jose Antonio Vargas says that Zuckerberg's demeanor is "a strange mixture of shy and cocky" and adds that Zuckerberg can "also come off as flip and condescending … but face to face he is often charming."[89] Author David Kirkpatrick maintains that "he may be a tad naïve, but he is simultaneously fearless, competitive, and supremely confident."[90] Facebook COO Sandberg finds him "funny, nice, and deeply caring, but most definitely shy."[91] During a talk he gave at the Computer History Museum in Mountain View, California, someone asked Zuckerberg if he was the same person in public as he was with his friends. Zuckerberg answered, "Yeah, same awkward person."[92]

Zuckerberg's Advice to Eighth Graders

On June 9, 2011, Mark Zuckerberg gave a speech to the graduating class at Belle Haven Community School in Menlo Park, California. He focused on overcoming the "I can't" attitude, noting that anything worth doing is difficult and that people should do what they love. He also emphasized the importance of relationships:

> A lot of the time the experts, the people who are supposed to be able to tell you what to do, will tell you that you can't do something even when you know you can. And a lot of the times, it's your friends and the people who are around you who trust you and who know you, who … tell you that you can do it. … Society [often focuses] on the one person, the athlete, the lead singer in the band, the person who started the company as the people who are the heroes. [But] no one ever does anything alone. People always do things with their friends … and it's those relationships that enable you to build awesome things.

Mark Zuckerberg. "Mark Zuckerberg's Speech to Eighth Graders at Belle Haven." Video. TechCrunch, June 9, 2011. http://techcrunch.com/2011/06/09/mark-zuckerberg-to-8th-graders-theres-no-shortcut.

The Giving Pledge

On December 8, 2010, three months after his *Oprah* appearance, Zuckerberg signed the Giving Pledge, a campaign that encourages the wealthiest people in the United States to commit to donating at least half their lifetime earnings to charity. Other signatories include Bill and Melinda Gates, George Lucas, and Zuckerberg's friend and Facebook cofounder Dustin Moskovitz. "People wait until late in their career to give back," said Zuckerberg in his pledge letter. "But why wait when there is so much to be done?"[93] Again, some critics suspected Zuckerberg's charity was self-focused. Carl Mortished of the *Globe and Mail* wrote, "I wish [Zuckerberg] would do something less egotistical and more useful to the world's poor and disadvantaged. ... I would rather he invested ... in some amazing new enterprise. Walk away from Facebook and start again."[94]

While Zuckerberg has no plans to walk away from Facebook, he has contributed to other enterprises, such as the Diaspora project, an open-source social network started by four college students at New York University. Although it is considered a Facebook competitor, Zuckerberg claims that he appreciates Diaspora's drive to change the world: "I think it's cool people are trying to do it. I see a little of myself in them. It's just their approach that the world could be better and saying 'We should try to do it.'"[95]

Zuckerberg has also become a member of Google Plus, another directly competing social network that emerged in 2011. Somewhat ironically, he quickly became the most followed member on Google Plus. His bare-bones profile initially proclaimed he was a male from Palo Alto who likes to make things. Zuckerberg sees the emergence of alternative social networks as a healthy and positive challenge: "I view a lot of this as validation as to how the next five years are going to play out." Implying that he is not overly concerned about the Internet's most popular search engine as a network competitor, he maintains: "Our job is to stay focused."[96]

Unique Personal Challenges

Zuckerberg enjoys setting distinctive yearly challenges for himself. In 2009, for example, he wore a tie every day, claiming that he wanted to express what an important and serious a year it was for Facebook. In 2010 he decided to start learning Mandarin Chinese—partly in preparation for a two-week trip to China that December, a gift from his girlfriend, Chan. As he mentioned on Facebook, "some members of my girlfriend's family only speak Chinese and I want to be able to talk with them."[97]

Like other Facebook users, Zuckerberg offers commentary and information on his personal life on his own Facebook page.

In 2011 Zuckerberg pledged to eat meat only from animals he has personally slaughtered. While claiming to be "basically" a vegetarian, Zuckerberg says that he has nothing against eating meat as long as one takes responsibility for the animal's death: "Many people forget that a living being has to die for you to eat meat, so my goal revolves around not letting myself forget that and being thankful for what I have." Beginning with lobsters, he has gone on to kill chickens, pigs, and goats—by cutting their throats with a knife, which is considered the most humane way to slaughter an animal. Zuckerberg takes the killed animals to a butcher so they can be cut into parts for eating. He once ate a chicken—heart and liver included—used the feet to make soup stock, and posted a photo of the bird on Facebook alongside a list of the dishes he made from it. "So far, this has been a good experience," Zuckerberg wrote in an explanatory e-mail to *Fortune* magazine. "I'm eating a lot of healthier foods and I've learned a lot about sustainable farming and raising of animals."[98]

Zuckerberg includes "eliminating desire" and "minimalism" as "interests" on his Facebook profile. He also practices meditation. In reference to "eliminating desire," Zuckerberg once jokingly commented to an interviewer, "I think it's probably Buddhist?"[99] Although raised Jewish, Zuckerberg today claims to be an atheist. Some commentators have suggested that his spiritual orientation is akin to Zen, with its emphasis on simplicity, mindfulness, and inner peace.

Hacker Values

Zuckerberg has also listed "breaking things" and "making things"[100] as "likes" on his profile. These contrasting elements are a reflection of Zuckerberg's hacker philosophy—a recognition that the cleverness required to break into a computer system can also be applied to creating innovative new technologies. It serves as a tongue-in-cheek reminder that Facebook itself emerged out of an all-night hacking spree in a dorm room. "Move Fast and Break Things" remains one of Facebook's company slogans—a statement that is painted on the walls of its office headquarters.

In a letter included as part of Facebook's February 2012 initial public offering, Zuckerberg highlighted a perspective that he calls the Hacker Way. Contending that hacking has been given an unfairly negative connotation in the media, Zuckerberg writes: "In reality, hacking just means building something quickly or testing the boundaries of what can be done. Like most things, it can be used for good or bad, but the vast majority of hackers I've met tend to be idealistic people who want to have a positive impact on the world." In his opinion the Hacker Way is "an approach to building that involves continuous improvement. ... Hackers believe that something can always be better ... often in the face of people who say it's impossible or are content with the status quo."[101]

Thus, hacking has become a company value, a Facebook rule to live by. Facebook hosts "hackathons" every six to eight weeks in which participants have one night to dream up and complete

Facebook's embrace of hacker culture is literally built into its headquarters, as an aerial shot of a courtyard emblazoned with the word "hack" demonstrates.

a project. The company provides food, music, and beer. "That's part of ... Facebook now," says Zuckerberg. "We have a big belief in moving fast, pushing boundaries, saying that it's OK to break things. It's definitely very core to my personality."[102]

An Introvert in a Very Public Role

Another contradiction that Zuckerberg embodies is that of a private person in the business of making the world a more public and transparent place. Temperamentally, Zuckerberg is not attracted to the limelight—televised interviews with him are rare—but his role as CEO of Facebook increasingly draws the attention of the media and the worlds of business and technology. Since 2010 he has made more public appearances and has been interviewed in print and on television. Dialogues with Zuckerberg have appeared in the *New Yorker*, *Time*, *Newsweek*, *Wired*, Jeff Jarvis's book *Public Parts*, and David Kirkpatrick's *The Facebook Effect*. He has been

Zuckerberg looks on as President Barack Obama holds a live town hall meeting through Facebook at the company's headquarters in 2011.

interviewed on *60 Minutes*, *ABC World News with Diane Sawyer*, and *Charlie Rose*.

In some of his earliest videotaped interviews, Zuckerberg appears anxious and sweaty; recently he seems more comfortable with audiences. He told one interviewer, "I usually don't like things that are too much about me."[103] On April 20, 2011, Barack Obama was the first U.S. president to hold a live town hall meeting through Facebook. Zuckerberg spoke very quickly during his introduction of Obama, then paused to take a breath, chuckled, and openly admitted his nervousness.

Zuckerberg has had to deal with another downside of fame. In February 2011 he took out a restraining order against Pradeep Manukonda, a stalker who showed up at Facebook's offices and at Zuckerberg's home to ask for money for his allegedly financially strapped family. Manukonda used threatening language against Zuckerberg and his girlfriend and sister. Accordingly, the home

Facebook and the Arab Spring

Facebook played a significant role in the Arab Spring, the unprecedented wave of demonstrations and protests that swept through several Arab nations during 2011 and 2012. Activists' increasing reliance on social networks, commentators claimed, was instrumental in mobilizing people, shaping opinions, and effecting change—including the toppling of regimes in Tunisia, Egypt, and Libya. Many of the initial calls for protest occurred on Facebook.

An Egyptian man holds a sign praising Facebook during a protest in Cairo's Tahrir Square in February 2011.

However, during the e-G8 Forum on May 25, 2011, in Paris, France, Mark Zuckerberg downplayed the role of Facebook:

> It would be extremely arrogant for any tech company to claim any meaningful role. ... Facebook was neither necessary nor sufficient for any of those things to happen. I do think over time the Internet is playing a role in making it so people can communicate more effectively, and that probably does help to organize some of these things. [But] if it weren't Facebook it would be something else.

Mark Zuckerberg. Speech at e-G8 Forum in Paris, France. May 25, 2011.

he purchased in Palo Alto in May 2011 is surrounded by security cameras and other protections.

A More Open and Connected World

Zuckerberg has always said that his goal in cofounding Facebook was to provide tools that help people share and connect with each other more—in user-defined ways that can range from the broadly communal to the confidential. Yet Facebook frequently falters at this when new features are added or when the website is restructured, leaving members confused over which posts are public or private. And many critics say that Facebook's profits depend on making private moments public and on people sharing too much. Dan Fletcher writes in *Time* magazine:

> Facebook is rich in intimate opportunities—you can share your niece's first steps there or mourn the death of a close friend—but the company is making money because you are, on some level, broadcasting those moments online. The feelings you experience on Facebook are heartfelt; the data you're providing feeds a bottom line. ...

Facebook's home page contains a simple statement summarizing the company's mission of helping people connect and share with others.

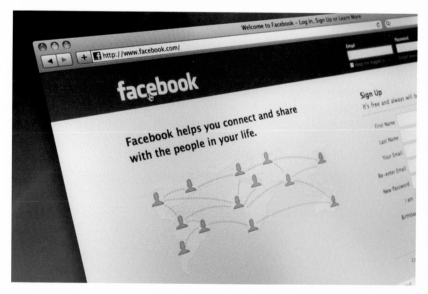

The willingness of Facebook's users to share and overshare … is critical to its success.[104]

Yet Zuckerberg maintains he is more interested in quality than in quantity when it comes to how people interact on the social network. "We're not trying to make it so that people spend a lot more time on Facebook," he says, "we're trying to make it so that the time you spend on Facebook is so valuable that you want to keep on coming back every day."[105] Rather than publicizing people's private lives, his aim is to create more bridges between people. Increased connectedness, he believes, leads to greater empathy, transparency, trust, and integrity—and ultimately, a more open and enlightened world. Jarvis, author of *Public Parts*, agrees: "[Zuckerberg] started Facebook … not, as [some] say, because he is trying to force us into the public. He contends he is creating the tools that help people do what they naturally want to do but couldn't do before. In his view, he's not changing human nature. He's enabling it."[106]

Introduction: A Rogue Who Builds Bridges

1. Mark Zuckerberg. "Mark Zuckerberg's Speech to Eighth Graders at Belle Haven." Video. TechCrunch, June 9, 2011. http://techcrunch.com/2011/06/09/mark-zuckerberg-to-8th-graders-theres-no-shortcuts.
2. Quoted in Jeff Jarvis. *Public Parts: How Sharing in the Digital Age Improves the Way We Work and Live*. New York: Simon and Schuster, 2011, p. 17.
3. Quoted in CNBC. *Mark Zuckerberg: Inside Facebook*. Documentary. January 26, 2012.
4. Quoted in Chris Sorenson. "The Anti-hero: A Genius Web Visionary, or a Rogue Who's Cashed In on the Folly of Others? Either Way It Was Mark Zuckerberg's Year in the Public Eye." *Maclean's*, December 13, 2010, p. 120.
5. Quoted in CNBC. *Mark Zuckerberg*.

Chapter 1: Boy Wonder

6. Quoted in Nathaniel Popper. "Meet Edward Zuckerberg, Tech-Savvy Dentist (and Mark's Father)." *Los Angeles Times*, March 30, 2011. http://articles.latimes.com/2011/mar/30/business/la-fi-zuckerberg-father-20110330.
7. Quoted in Popper. "Meet Edward Zuckerberg, Tech-Savvy Dentist (and Mark's Father)."
8. Quoted in Lev Grossman. "Person of the Year 2010: Mark Zuckerberg." *Time*, December 15, 2010. www.time.com/time/specials/packages/article/0,28804,2036683_2037183_2037185,00.html.
9. Quoted in Beth J. Harpaz. "Mark Zuckerberg's Father Discusses Facebook CEO's Upbringing." *Huffington Post*,

February 4, 2011. www.huffingtonpost.com/2011/02/04/mark-zuckerberg-father-edward_n_818892.html.

10. Quoted in Popper. "Meet Edward Zuckerberg, Tech-Savvy Dentist (and Mark's Father)."

11. Quoted in Harpaz. "Mark Zuckerberg's Father Discusses Facebook CEO's Upbringing."

12. Quoted in Jose Antonio Vargas. "The Face of Facebook." *New Yorker*, September 20, 2010. www.newyorker.com/reporting/2010/09/20/100920fa_fact_vargas.

13. Quoted in Vargas. "The Face of Facebook."

14. Quoted in Grossman. "Person of the Year 2010."

15. Quoted in Grossman. "Person of the Year 2010."

16. Quoted in Vargas. "The Face of Facebook."

17. Quoted in Daniel Alef. *Mark Zuckerberg: The Face Behind Facebook and Social Networking*. Santa Barbara, CA: Titans of Fortune, 2010. Kindle edition.

18. Quoted in Vargas. "The Face of Facebook."

19. Vargas. "The Face of Facebook."

20. Quoted in Claire Hoffman. "The Battle for Facebook." *Rolling Stone*, September 15, 2010. www.rollingstone.com/culture/news/the-battle-for-facebook-20100915.

21. Steffan Antonas. "Did Mark Zuckerberg's Inspiration for Facebook Come Before Harvard?" ReadWriteWeb, May 10, 2009. www.readwriteweb.com/archives/mark_zuckerberg_inspiration_for_facebook_before_harvard.php.

22. Antonas. "Did Mark Zuckerberg's Inspiration for Facebook Come Before Harvard?"

23. Phillips Exeter Academy Website. "Computer Science." www.exeter.edu/academics/72_6506.aspx.

24. Quoted in Alef. *Mark Zuckerberg*.

25. Quoted in Alef. *Mark Zuckerberg*.

26. Quoted in Michael M. Grynbaum. "Mark E. Zuckerberg '06: The Whiz Behind Thefacebook.com." *Harvard Crimson*, June 10, 2004. www.thecrimson.com/article/2004/6/10/mark-e-zuckerberg-06-the-whiz.

Chapter 2: Hacking and High Jinks at Harvard

27. Quoted in David Kirkpatrick. *The Facebook Effect: The Inside Story of the Company That Is Connecting the World.* New York: Simon & Schuster, 2010, p. 20.
28. Quoted in Vargas. "The Face of Facebook."
29. Kirkpatrick. *The Facebook Effect*, p. 21.
30. Quoted in Kirkpatrick. *The Facebook Effect*, p. 22.
31. Quoted in Kirkpatrick. *The Facebook Effect*, p. 19.
32. Quoted in Kirkpatrick. *The Facebook Effect*, p. 26.
33. Quoted in Kirkpatrick. *The Facebook Effect*, p. 20.
34. Quoted in Ben Mezrich. *The Accidental Billionaires: The Founding of Facebook.* New York: Anchor, 2009, p. 42.
35. Quoted in Mezrich. *The Accidental Billionaires*, p. 43.
36. Quoted in Mezrich. *The Accidental Billionaires*, p. 49.
37. Quoted in Bari M. Schwartz. "Hot or Not? Website Briefly Judges Looks." *Harvard Crimson*, November 4, 2003. www.thecrimson.com/article/2003/11/4/hot-or-not-website-briefly-judges.
38. Quoted in Kirkpatrick. *The Facebook Effect*, p. 25.
39. *Harvard Crimson.* "Put Online a Happy Face." December 11, 2003. www.thecrimson.com/article/2003/12/11/put-online-a-happy-face-after.
40. Sarah E.F. Milov. "Sociology of Thefacebook.com." *Harvard Crimson*, March 1, 2004. www.thecrimson.com/article/2004/3/18/sociology-of-thefacebookcom-at-harvard-fun.
41. Quoted in Hoffman. "The Battle for Facebook."
42. Quoted in Grynbaum. "Mark E. Zuckerberg '06: The Whiz Behind Thefacebook.com."
43. Alan J. Tabak. "Hundreds Register for New Facebook Website." *Harvard Crimson*, February 9, 2004. www.thecrimson.com/article/2004/2/9/hundreds-register-for-new-facebook-website.
44. Quoted in Timothy J. McGinn. "Online Facebooks Duel Over Tangled Web of Authorship." *Harvard Crimson*, May 28,

2004. www.thecrimson.com/article/2004/5/28/online-facebooks-duel-over-tangled-web.

45. Quoted in McGinn. "Online Facebooks Duel Over Tangled Web of Authorship."
46. Quoted in Nicholas Carson. "At Last—the Full Story of How Facebook Was Founded." *Business Insider*, March 5, 2010. www.businessinsider.com/how-facebook-was-founded-2010-3.
47. Quoted in Hoffman. "The Battle for Facebook."
48. Quoted in Hoffman. "The Battle for Facebook."

Chapter 3: Building a Social Network

49. Quoted in Alef. *Mark Zuckerberg*.
50. Quoted in Alef. *Mark Zuckerberg*.
51. Quoted in Kirkpatrick. *The Facebook Effect*, p. 47.
52. Quoted in Kirkpatrick. *The Facebook Effect*, p. 53.
53. Quoted in Kirkpatrick. *The Facebook Effect*, p. 58.
54. Kirkpatrick. *The Facebook Effect*, p. 49.
55. Quoted in Kirkpatrick. *The Facebook Effect*, p. 52.
56. Quoted in Kirkpatrick. *The Facebook Effect*, p. 60.
57. Quoted in Kirkpatrick. *The Facebook Effect*, p. 123.
58. Quoted in Ellen McGirt. "Facebook's Mark Zuckerberg. Hacker. Dropout. CEO." *Fast Company*, May 1, 2007. www.fastcompany.com/magazine/115/open_features-hacker-dropout-ceo.html.

Chapter 4: Triumph and Controversy

59. Quoted in Kirkpatrick. *The Facebook Effect*, p. 149.
60. Quoted in Kirkpatrick. *The Facebook Effect*, p. 190.
61. Quoted in Brittney Farb. "Students Speak Out Against Facebook Feed." *Student Life*, September 8, 2006. www.studlife.com/archives/News/2006/09/08/StudentsspeakoutagainstFacebookfeed.
62. Quoted in Kirkpatrick. *The Facebook Effect*, pp. 191–192.

63. Quoted in U.S. Securities and Exchange Commission. Form S-1 Registration Statement. February 12, 2012. www.sec.gov/Archives/edgar/data/1326801/000119312512034517/d287954ds1.htm.
64. Quoted in Kirkpatrick. *The Facebook Effect*, p. 198.
65. Quoted in CNBC. *Mark Zuckerberg*.
66. Quoted in CNBC. *Mark Zuckerberg*.
67. Josh Quittner. "RIP Facebook?" *Fortune*, December 4, 2007. http://tech.fortune.cnn.com/2007/12/04/rip-facebook.
68. Mark Zuckerberg. "Thoughts on Beacon." *The Facebook Blog*, December 5, 2007. https://blog.facebook.com/blog.php%3Fpost%3D7584397130.
69. Quoted in Carson. "At Last—the Full Story of How Facebook Was Founded."
70. Quoted in Vargas. "The Face of Facebook."
71. Quoted in Vargas. "The Face of Facebook."
72. Quoted in Vargas. "The Face of Facebook."
73. Quoted in Ina Fried. "Zuckerberg in the Hot Seat at D8." CNET News, June 2, 2010. http://news.cnet.com/8301-13860_3-20006653-56.html?tag=mncol;title.
74. Quoted in *The Oprah Winfrey Show*. CBS, September 24, 2010.
75. Quoted in Finlo Rohrer. "Is the Facebook Movie the Truth About Mark Zuckerberg?" BBC News, September 30, 2010. www.bbc.co.uk/news/world-us-canada-11437873.
76. Quoted in *Saturday Night Live*. "Jesse Eisenberg Monologue." NBC.com, January 29, 2011. www.nbc.com/saturday-night-live/video/jesse-eisenberg-monologue/1279517.

Chapter 5: The Frugal Billionaire

77. Quoted in Grynbaum. "Mark E. Zuckerberg '06."
78. Quoted in Vargas. "The Face of Facebook."
79. Quoted in Mary Phillips-Sandy. "Meet Priscilla Chan, Mark Zuckerberg's No-Nonsense Girlfriend." AOL News, February 8, 2011. www.aolnews.com/2011/02/08/meet-priscilla-chan-mark-zuckerbergs-no-nonsense-girlfriend.

80. Quoted in Vargas. "The Face of Facebook."

81. John Stevens. "Finally! Facebook Founder Mark Zuckerberg Buys His Very First Home Three Years After Becoming World's Youngest Billionaire." *Mail Online*, May 6, 2011. www .dailymail.co.uk/news/article-1384071/Facebook-founder-Mark-Zuckerberg-buys-home.html#ixzz1LaYbM7DQ.

82. Jessica Guynn. "Zuckerberg's Palo Alto Home Still Well Below His Means." *Los Angeles Times*, May 6, 2011. www .latimes.com/business/la-fi-0506-zuckerberg-house-20110506,0,555362.story.

83. TMZ. "Zuckerberg's New Home—You Paid $7 Mil for That?" www.tmz.com/2011/05/06/mark-zuckerberg-7-million-house-that-facebook-bought-palo-alto-girlfriend-saltwater-pool-5-bedrooms-not-renting/#.T0Rsb4fCmf4.

84. Quoted in *The Oprah Winfrey Show*.

85. Mark Zuckerberg. "Blog Post from Mark Zuckerberg." Startup: Education, Facebook. September 24, 2010. www .facebook.com/note.php?note_id=116078918450633.

86. Josh Duboff. "Mark Zuckerberg's Well-Timed $100 Million Donation to Newark Public Schools." *New York*, September 22, 2010. http://nymag.com/daily/intel/2010/09/mark_zuckerberg_to_give_100_mi.html.

87. Robert Frank. "Mark Zuckerberg: An Embarrassment of Riches." *The Wealth Report* (blog). *Wall Street Journal*, September 23, 2010. http://blogs.wsj.com/wealth/2010/09/23/mark-zuckerberg-an-embarrassment-of-riches.

88. Quoted in *The Oprah Winfrey Show*.

89. Vargas. "The Face of Facebook."

90. Kirkpatrick. *The Facebook Effect*, p. 314.

91. Quoted in Sorenson. "The Anti-hero," *Academic OneFile*. Web. 14 May 2012.

92. Quoted in Vargas. "The Face of Facebook."

93. Quoted in Giving Pledge. "Seventeen More U.S. Families Take Giving Pledge." Press release. December 8, 2010. http://givingpledge.org/Content/media/PressRelease_12_8.pdf.

94. Carl Mortished. "Tycoons, Give Your Billions to Businesses, Not Charity." *Toronto Globe and Mail*, December 9, 2010.

www.theglobeandmail.com/report-on-business/economy/economy-lab/carl-mortished/tycoons-give-your-billions-to-businesses-not-charity/article1830987.

95. Quoted in Ryan Singel. "Mark Zuckerberg: I Donated to Open Source, Facebook Competitor." *Wired*, May 28, 2010. www.wired.com/epicenter/2010/05/zuckerberg-interview.

96. Quoted in Goncarlo Ribero. "Facebook CEO Mark Zuckerberg on Google+: Been There, Done That." *Redmond Pie*, July 7, 2011. www.redmondpie.com/facebooks-ceo-mark-zuckerberg-on-google-been-there-done-that.

97. Mark Zuckerberg's Facebook Timeline, posted January 1, 2010. www.facebook.com/zuck.

98. Quoted in Patricia Sellers. "Eating Only What He Kills (and Yes, We Do Mean Literally...)." *Postcards* (blog). *Fortune*, May 26, 2011. http://postcards.blogs.fortune.cnn.com/2011/05/26/mark-zuckerbergs-new-challenge-eating-only-what-he-kills.

99. Quoted in Grossman. "Person of the Year 2010."

100. Mark Zuckerberg's Facebook Profile, accessed May 14, 2012. www.facebook.com/zuck.

101. Quoted in U.S. Securities and Exchange Commission. Form S-1 Registration Statement.

102. Quoted in Steven Levy. "Geek Power: Steven Levy Revisits Tech Titans, Hackers, Idealists." *Wired*, May 2010. www.wired.com/magazine/2010/04/ff_hackers/all/1.

103. Quoted in Grossman. "Person of the Year 2010."

104. Dan Fletcher. "How Facebook Is Redefining Privacy." *Time*, May 20, 2010. www.time.com/time/magazine/article/0,9171,1990798,00.html.

105. Quoted in CNBC. *Mark Zuckerberg*.

106. Jarvis. *Public Parts*, p. 17.

1984

Mark Elliott Zuckerberg is born on May 14 to Edward and Karen Zuckerberg.

1995

Receives tutoring in computer programming from a software developer; takes graduate level computer courses at Mercy College.

1996

Creates Zucknet, a messaging program that connects all the computers in the Zuckerberg household.

1998

Attends Ardsley High School, where he excels in classics.

2000

Transfers to Phillips Exeter Academy.

2001–2002

With classmate Adam D'Angelo, develops Synapse Media Player for a senior project; turns down several software companies' offers of millions of dollars for Synapse.

2002

Enters Harvard University as a double major in psychology and computer science.

2003

Creates Course Match; hacks into the Harvard computer system and uses that data to create Facemash; approached by Divya Narendra, Tyler Winklevoss, and Cameron Winklevoss to write code for Harvard Connection.

2004

Launches TheFacebook from his dorm room; meets Napster cofounder Sean Parker, who suggests development ideas for TheFacebook; forms TheFacebook LLC as a partnership with Eduardo Saverin and Dustin Moskovitz; moves TheFacebook to Silicon Valley; Narendra and the Winklevoss brothers sue TheFacebook; TheFacebook's membership reaches 1 million.

2005

Fires Saverin; Accel Partners invests $12.7 million in TheFacebook, and Zuckerberg, with three of the five board seats, maintains control of the company; TheFacebook becomes Facebook; Facebook's membership reaches 5 million.

2007

Zuckerberg launches Facebook Platform; Microsoft invests $240 million in Facebook, valuing the company at $15 billion; Facebook's membership grows to more than 50 million; Zuckerberg launches Beacon, which he later redesigns to allow members to opt out.

2008

Settles Narendra and the Winklevoss brothers lawsuit for an estimated $65 million; Saverin's lawsuit against Zuckerberg and Facebook is settled out of court for an undetermined amount.

2010

Facebook's membership reaches more than 500 million; Zuckerberg announces his $100 million donation to the Newark public school system; *The Social Network* film is released and Zuckerberg claims that it is a largely inaccurate account of what happened; plays himself in an episode of *The Simpsons*; interviews former U.S. president George W. Bush on Facebook; signs the Giving Pledge, promising to donate most of his lifetime earnings to charity; *Vanity Fair* ranks Zuckerberg as number one on its list of Top One Hundred Most Influential People of the Digital Age; he is named *Time* magazine's Person of the Year.

2011

Makes a surprise appearance on *Saturday Night Live*; Barack Obama becomes the first U.S. president to hold a national town hall meeting on Facebook; Zuckerberg purchases a $7 million home in Palo Alto, California.

2012

Facebook's membership reaches more than 800 million; Facebook files an initial public offering; *Forbes* magazine lists Zuckerberg as the 14th richest American, with a personal wealth estimated at $17.5 billion; married girlfriend Priscilla Chan on May 19.

Books

Judy L. Hasday. *Facebook and Mark Zuckerberg*. Greensboro, NC: Morgan Reynolds, 2011. Presents a portrait of Zuckerberg as a business and technology leader.

Jeff Jarvis. *Public Parts: How Sharing in the Digital Age Improves the Way We Work and Live*. New York: Simon and Schuster, 2011. This author examines the benefits and drawbacks of living a life in which increasingly more information is shared. Includes an interview with Zuckerberg.

David Kirkpatrick. *The Facebook Effect: The Inside Story of the Company That Is Connecting the World*. New York: Simon and Schuster, 2011. An authorized and detailed account of the founding and evolution of Facebook. It includes discussions with Mark Zuckerberg, Sean Parker, and other Facebook board members and employees.

Marcia Amidon Lusted. *Mark Zuckerberg: Facebook Creator*. Minneapolis, MN: Abdo, 2011. A biography of Zuckerberg written specifically for teen audiences.

Jerome Maida and Fritz Saalfeld. *Mark Zuckerberg: Creator of Facebook GN*. Beverly Hills, CA: Bluewater, 2012. The story of how Zuckerberg became the youngest billionaire in the world—presented in comic book form.

Ben Mezrich. *The Accidental Billionaires: The Founding of Facebook*. New York: Anchor, 2009. An unauthorized, controversial depiction of Zuckerberg's college life and Facebook's early days, this book provided the inspiration for the movie *The Social Network*.

Periodicals

Jeremy Borin. "Facebook Founder Makes Recruiting Call." *Pittsburgh Tribune-Review*, November 9, 2011.

John Cassidy. "ME MEDIA." *New Yorker*, May 15, 2006.

Sally Deneen. "The Facebook Age: What Began as a Lark in Mark Zuckerberg's Dorm Room Has Changed the Way People Relate to One Another." *Success*, May 2011.

Kristi Oloffson. "The (True?) Story Behind Facebook's Founding." *Time*, July 15, 2009.

Mandy Stadtmiller. "Facebook's Worst Enemies." *New York Post*, September 15, 2010.

Chris Sorenson. "The Anti-hero: A Genius Web Visionary, or a Rogue Who's Cashed In on the Folly of Others? Either Way It Was Mark Zuckerberg's Year in the Public Eye." *Maclean's*, December 13, 2010.

Jose Antonio Vargas. "The Face of Facebook." *New Yorker*, September 20, 2010.

Internet Sources

Chloe Albanesius. "Facebook 'Deceived' Users, FTC Finds." *PC Magazine*, November 29, 2011. www.pcmag.com/article2 /0,2817,2396992,00.asp?google_editors_picks=true.

Dan Fletcher. "How Facebook Is Redefining Privacy." *Time*, May 20, 2010. www.time.com/time/magazine/article /0,9171,1990798,00.html.

Claire Hoffman. "The Battle for Facebook." *Rolling Stone*, September 15, 2010. www.rollingstone.com/culture/news/the-battle-for-facebook-20100915.

David Kirkpatrick. "What's True in the Facebook Movie." *Daily Beast*, September 30, 2010. www.thedailybeast.com/articles /2010/09/30/the-facebook-and-zuckerberg-in-the-social-network-arent-real.html.

Dana Vachon. "The Code of the Winklevii." *Vanity Fair*, December 2011. www.vanityfair.com/business/features/ 2011/12/winklevosses-201112.

Websites

The Facebook Blog (http://blog.facebook.com). Facebook employees give firsthand accounts of new features, products, and goings-on at the company. An archive of blog posts sorted by topic and date is included.

Geek.com (www.geek.com). Offers an online resource guide and community for computer enthusiasts. Includes breaking news about personalities and products in the world of technology.

Inside Facebook (www.insidefacebook.com). An independent website that provides news and analysis on Facebook's global growth, corporate developments, and product innovations.

Quora (www.quora.com). Started by Adam D'Angelo, Zuckerberg's high school friend, Quora is a website that shares content from the web, answering specific questions asked by its members.

Mary E. Williams earned a master of fine arts degree from San Diego State University, where she studied comparative literature and creative writing. She writes and edits nonfiction books for young adults and is currently working on a memoir. Williams lives in San Marcos, California, with her husband, Kirk, and their two cats, Harpo and Kali. In her spare time she enjoys good books, movies, road trips, and conversations with far-flung friends through various social networks, including Facebook.

- -
B
ZUCKERBERG
W

Williams, Mary E.,
    1960-

Mark Zuckerberg.

$37.45

DATE			